Y0-BRX-867

Practical Suggestions
for Successful Ministry

Practical Suggestions for Successful Ministry

By
Dr. Frederick K.C. Price

Harrison House
Tulsa, Oklahoma

Unless otherwise indicated, all Scripture quotations are taken from the *King James Version* of the Bible.

Scripture quotations marked NAS are taken from the *New American Standard Bible.* Copyright © The Lockman Foundation 1960, 1962, 1963, 1968, 1971, 1972, 1973, 1975, 1977. Used by permission.

Practical Suggestions for Successful Ministry
ISBN 0-89274-880-X
Copyright © 1991 by Frederick K.C. Price
Crenshaw Christian Center
P. O. Box 90000
Los Angeles, California 90009

Published by Harrison House, Inc.
P. O. Box 35035
Tulsa, Oklahoma 74153

Printed in the United States of America. All rights reserved under International Copyright Law. Contents and/or cover may not be reproduced in whole or in part in any form without the express written consent of the Publisher.

Contents

Introduction

In 1980, while I was at a ministers' conference in the city of St. Louis, Missouri, the Lord gave me a special message, which involved living a successful Christian life.

The principles He shared with me will work for any Christian. However, I have prepared this book especially for those called to teach and preach the full counsel of God. Therefore, ministers of the Gospel are the ones to whom these principles and this book are addressed.

1
God Wants Us
To Be Victorious

Before elaborating on the principles of a successful ministry, I want to discuss some practical suggestions for living a victorious Christian life, because the Christian should not live haphazardly. His life should be lived solely on Bible doctrines. If one wants to be a total overcomer, the biblical principles that govern success have to be clearly understood and applied.

There are too many Christians, including some ministers, who have the mediocre mentality. That is a mentality of just doing what everyone else is doing. In other words, such a person is content to merely survive as a Christian and in ministry. But that is not how the Bible tells us to live.

For those called to full time ministry, I want to emphasize this: *If you are doing what God called you to do, what He has anointed you to do, what He has given you a vision to do, if you are doing all these things, then you are successful!*

You may never have a ministry of 500,000 or 25,000 members. But that is not the point. The point is that you are fulfilling what God has called you to do — and you know when you are and when you are not!

The first thing I want to do is to cover some Scriptures which illustrate that God wants us to be successful. Before beginning in the book of Joshua, however, here's a little background:

Moses was now dead. The children of Israel were perched on the far side of the Jordan River before entering into Canaan land. The first obstacle they had to face was the city of Jericho. Just prior to going across and into Jericho, God gave Joshua a commandment.

I believe this commandment has universal application that will work with the Old Covenant, the New Covenant, or whether you are a minister or a lay person. The principle works the same way.

Joshua 1:8

This book of the law shall not depart out of thy mouth (meaning should not stop speaking God's Word); **but thou shalt meditate therein day and night,** (that is a full-time job) **that thou mayest observe to do according to all that is written therein: for then thou shalt make thy way prosperous, and then thou shalt have good success.**

Notice what it says, **That thou mayest observe.** . . . But that does not mean to observe only, but, rather, **observe** *to do* **all that is written therein:**

The Commandment is:

1. *Do not let the Word out of your mouth.* In other words, do not stop speaking God's Word. That is the first thing you have to do.

2. *Meditate day and night.* That is the second most important thing.

3. *Observe.* That is the third most important thing; and

4. *TO DO;* THAT is the *sum total* and *most important part of all!*

God says, **for then** (notice the **then** does not come until after the four things are done) **thou shalt make thy way prosperous, and then thou shalt have good success.**

This tells me that God wants me to prosper. He wants me to be successful, not mediocre, not barely making it. God wants me to be on top!

Good Success, Bad Success
It Is Up To YOU!

Notice this very important statement: **For then THOU shalt make....** It does not say that THE LORD shall make. Too many ministers are waiting on the Lord to do something in their ministries.

No! God says if you are successful, it is *your* fault. If you are a failure, it is *your* fault. If you are mediocre, it is *your* fault — not God's fault, not the devil's fault, not the congregation's, nor the people's fault — but YOUR fault!

One translation says to have good success means **that thou shall deal wisely in the affairs of life.** I like what the *King James Bible* says, because I believe there is a revelation here. It says, **...then thou shalt have GOOD success.**

Why in the world would the Holy Spirit tell me I will have GOOD success? What other kind of success could you have but good? Why say "good" to distinguish from bad success? Because there is bad success!

What am I talking about when I say "bad" success? Success, by virtue of its definition, implies good — not a negative, but a positive. Yet, in the Book of Joshua, it says **good success,** because there are many people who have bad success.

In our society, we equate success with big bank accounts, big cars, big diamond rings, big houses, big wallets, and other material things that stand for success. However, there are many people who have all those things and still they have no peace.

They cannot sleep at night. They cannot eat certain foods because their stomachs are eaten up by ulcers caused by stress and worry. And they do not know who their friends are. They do not trust anyone; nevertheless, they have what is considered to be success in a material way.

Their success, in my opinion, is not good, but bad! Their children are running wild; sometimes the parents do not even know where their children are. Their sons are on drugs, their daughters are getting pregnant out of wedlock; yet they have all the money in the world and all the acclaim. But their success is bad, not good.

It thrills me to know that no one can compromise my success. If I succeed, it is because I do it. If I fail, it is because I do it. I cannot blame anyone but myself.

We understand God is our Source, but God is not doing anything in this earth realm, WE are — that is, the Body of Christ is! God works through the Body. He provides the power, the enabling ability, and the anointing to the Body, but it is the Body doing the work.

If I do not do something with my ministry or my life, then I am not going to succeed, because God is not a failure. There is no way God can fail. And there is too much failure in ministry — too many mediocre ministers. Some ministers remain mediocre throughout their lives, never really fulfilling what God has called them to do.

In Psalm 1, beginning with the first verse, this same principle is enunciated:

Psalm 1:1-3

Blessed is the man that walketh not in the counsel of the ungodly, nor standeth in the way of sinners, nor sitteth in the seat of the scornful.

But his delight is in the law of the Lord; and in his law doth he meditate day and night. (There's that day and night again.)

And he shall be like a tree planted by the rivers of water, that bringeth forth his fruit in his season; his

10

leaf also shall not wither; and whatsoever he doeth shall PROSPER.

Whatsoever he doeth shall prosper. That has to include ministry. Notice that the **shall prosper** comes *after* doing these other things. In other words, *we* have to meet the conditions. God cannot meet them for us. All the ingredients are already here for us to develop our own prosperity.

Think about it from this standpoint: Airplanes and 747 jumbo jets were in the Garden of Eden with Adam. Electric lights were in the Garden of Eden with Adam. Aerodynamics were in the Garden.

God did not all of a sudden push aerodynamics into the earth realm 50 or 60 years ago when Orville and Wilbur Wright made their first flight at Kitty Hawk. No! All the principles of flight and all of the materials needed to make an airplane were in the earth realm in the Garden of Eden, but no one knew it, because no one had discovered it yet. The point is that if man were ever to fly, it was up to man and not up to God.

If you succeed in ministry, it is not up to God, it is up to you. All of the ingredients for success are already here, and He has given you a plan to follow so that you can succeed. When you succeed, God succeeds. When you fail, God fails, because people cannot see God. They can only see His so-called representatives. If the representatives of God are failures, then in the eyes of the world, God is a failure.

God Needs Role Models

God needs role models, and ministers are to be God's role models. Unsaved people judge God by God's so-called people. That is why I made it up in my mind years ago that I was going to represent God on a level that would be above reproach. If any man rejected Jesus, it would not be because

11

I was so sloppily dressed, smelling bad, or driving some old beat up, broken down, junky car! I determined in my mind that I was going to represent God to the best of my ability.

I remember seeing insurance salesmen in my neighborhood when they used to go from house to house years ago selling insurance. They looked good. I see the Black Muslims out and about looking neat and clean, with trim haircuts and nice suits, all dressed up. I said to myself, "Why can't Christians represent God that way?"

That is another reason why I take care of my body. I am going to represent God in the best way I can. I am not going to be some fat preacher with 99 ballpoint pens in my top pocket, looking tattered and torn!

If this fits you, and you don't like what I am saying, CHANGE IT! You are the only one who can — God won't!

2

The Word of Faith
Is the Key to Success

Romans 1:17

For therein is the righteousness of God revealed from faith to faith: As it is written, The just shall live by faith.

"The just" means those who have been "declared righteous" shall live by faith. The Word of Faith is what will allow us to be successful, because FAITH is the KEY that unlocks the door.

Once a person becomes a Christian, the most important thing he or she needs to learn is how to walk by faith, because everything else in the Christian life operates by faith. EVERYTHING! That is why Satan fights the faith message so much.

There is no subject more important than faith once a person is born again. To the sinner, the most important subject is Jesus — salvation. Once he gets saved, the most important subject becomes the Word of Faith.

Many times people get filled with the Holy Spirit right after they receive Christ as their Savior. A great number of these people still have a problem with the baptism with the Holy Spirit because they don't understand that the whole premise of the infilling with the Holy Spirit operates by faith.

They go by how they feel. If they did not get the feeling that they thought they should have received, they go for

13

the next six years doubting whether they are really filled with the Holy Spirit. If they had known how to operate by faith, they would not have had a problem with their emotions and feelings.

Love Is Not More Important Than Faith

There is nothing you can name that is more important than faith once a person gets saved! And don't tell me *love!*

Love is not the most important thing. It IS important, of course, but it is not the most important — faith is!!

Some Christians have problems interacting with other people because they do not feel like loving them. I do not blame them, because everyone is not lovable, and unless you know how to walk by faith, there is no way to be able to relate to them in love.

I know that the Bible says that faith worketh by love, which simply means that the motivation for my faith operating ought to be love. However, I have news for you; even though it is not written, *love works by faith!* You have to love some people by faith, because everyone is not lovable.

I know that the last verse of First Corinthians 13 (NAS) says, **But now abide faith, hope, love, these three; but the greatest of these is love (charity** KJV). Yes, the greatest is love, right there where it says it is. Leave it there! Do not pull it out of First Corinthians 13 and apply it to John, Chapter 1, or Ephesians, Chapter 6, or Galatians, Chapter 4. Leave it in the 13th Chapter of First Corinthians. That is where it belongs — sandwiched right there in the middle between Chapter 12 and Chapter 14!

Love is the MOTIVE! It is the greatest reason for speaking with tongues and not sounding like a clanging cymbal. It is the greatest reason for operating by faith and seeing the sick healed, but it is not the greatest thing *by itself*. It is the greatest motivator.

Though I speak with tongues of men and angels and have not charity (love), Paul did not say that the tongues were not genuine, he just said, *without* love, you sound **like a tinkling cymbal and a sounding brass.**

He did not say you were not speaking with tongues. He did not say speaking with tongues was not legitimate. He did not say tongues were not coming out of your spirit. He just said it did not sound very edifying without being motivated by love. It just sounded like a clanging gong, but he did not say it was not the real thing.

Though I give my body to be burned and have not charity (love), **it profiteth me nothing.** He did not say that giving myself did not produce a result. Paul just said, it does not profit *me* anything personally. I should not do what I am doing because I have great faith. I should be doing what I am doing *because I love.*

Now abide faith, hope, love, these three; but the greatest of these is love. Love could not be the greatest thing by itself. If love were the greatest thing, then Hebrews 11:6 should say, **But without love it is impossible to please God.** It does not say a thing about love, but it does say, **Without faith, it is** *impossible* (that means NOT POSSIBLE; that means there is no way) **to please God.**

The Bible does not say all things are possible to him that loveth. But it does say, **All things are possible to him that believeth** (Mark 9:23).

I am in no way diminishing love, but we need to keep it where it belongs. We should not try to make it a panacea for everything, because it will not work. Love is what moves or motivates me to do certain things, and in that sense, there is nothing greater than love, because the love of God by the Holy Ghost has been shed abroad in the hearts of those who have been born again. (Rom. 5:5.)

With all of that in mind, once a person is saved, the most important thing is for him to learn how to operate by faith, because everything else he will do spiritually in life will be predicated on knowing how to operate by faith.

Not knowing how to operate by faith is why people have the problems they do. They are having problems because they are doing things in their own strengths, in their own abilities, in their own smarts, in their own academics, in their own feelings and emotions, and IT WON'T WORK! When you do it by faith, you do not have any problems, no challenges, because it is not based on a feeling.

It does not matter how you respond to me. I love you by faith according to the Word of God, so your response is irrelevant and immaterial. It does not make any difference what you do to me; you can spit in my face, and I will still love you. Not because I feel like it, but because I have a commandment from God, and I have the ability to do it by the Spirit of God by faith.

3
Walking by Faith — A Way of Life

The just shall live by faith. (Rom. 1:17.) Consequently, faith is a way of life. It is the way we live — not a magic wand. It is a lifestyle, the God-kind of life! Too many Christians try to use faith as a gimmick, an Aladdin's Lamp. "Genie, Genie, come out and give me a new Cadillac." "Genie, Genie, I want a yacht." "Genie, Genie, come out and give me a townhouse."

No! No! No! Faith is not a magic wand! You should be living by faith 24 hours a day, seven days a week, 365 1/4 days as the earth orbits the sun — faith is not something you just use as a parachute when you have a problem.

2 Corinthians 5:7

For we walk by FAITH, not by sight.

It is not like seeing with your eyes. This scripture is talking about the difference between walking by the things of the Spirit of God, which operates by faith, or walking by what your five senses tell you. I like to paraphrase this verse like this: *We walk by the Word and not by our senses.*

Romans 10:17 says:

Faith cometh by hearing, and hearing by the word of God.

If the Word of God is not heard, faith will not come. If faith cometh, then faith was not there before it cometh, or it would not have to come there.

17

Faith and the Word of God are synonymous terms. You cannot have one without the other. I like to think of faith and the Word like wet with the water. If you get the water, you get the wet, because wet is a characteristic of water. You cannot go to a restaurant and order a glass of water and say, "Hold the wet." You could order a hamburger and say, "Hold the onions." But you cannot say, "Bring me some water and hold the wet," because wet goes with the water.

Faith goes with the proclaimed Word of God. That is why Jesus said in Mark 16:15, **Go ye into all the world, and preach the gospel to every creature.** Why, Jesus? Because, *faith comes by hearing, and hearing by the Word of God.* If you do not go preach, faith cannot come. If faith cannot come, people cannot believe. If they cannot believe, they cannot get saved. If they cannot get saved, they are going to hell. Therefore, our job is to preach the Word, so that faith can come, so that people can hear and believe.

In many churches today, the Word is not being taught, and that is why many people are not experiencing the supernatural manifestations of the Spirit. Faith has to be generated in order for the Spirit to confirm the Word.

Nothing was happening in the church that I pastored years ago before I found out how to walk by the Word. God only confirms His Word.

Mark 16:20 says, **And they went forth, and preached every where, the Lord working with them, and confirming the word with signs following.** He did not confirm *them;* He confirmed the Word with signs following. You do not get the signs first, and then present His Word. You first present His Word, and the signs will follow. Signs are the natural outcome of the Word being taught.

No Seed Planted — No Harvest

If you want spiritual things to work, you are going to have to preach spiritual things. You want people to give?

You are going to have to preach on giving — not as a gimmick — but as a way of life that conforms to the principles of the Word of God.

God wants to bless His children, and when churches do not let them give, He cannot bless them. According to God's plan, the primary way we get blessed is by giving. It is the law of sowing and reaping. If you do not sow any seeds, you do not get any harvest. It is just that simple! Consequently, for that law to work in the Body of Christ, ministers of God *have* to preach it.

We have a responsibility to teach the people. If we want healing to work in our ministries, we have to preach on it.

In the four denominations that I used to belong to, we never had any supernatural manifestations. No one ever got healed. We had plenty of sick folk, but the reason why no one ever received healing was because no one ever preached the Word on divine healing. There was not any faith in the congregation for it. We were waiting on God, and God was waiting on *us*: "Well, I'll believe in healing when I see somebody get healed." And God was saying, "Well, I will do it, if you believe it."

God wants us to succeed, but we do it by faith. Once the faith principles are comprehended, we can then move on from there to achieve God's best. On the following pages, I have provided ten points that, along with faith, will produce fruitful results.

4

Ten Practical Suggestions
for Successful Ministry

#1
Living a Disciplined Life
(1 Corinthians 9:27)

No one can be successful in ministry who is undisciplined. There are too many undisciplined pastors, too many undisciplined evangelists, too many undisciplined ministers of the Gospel! To be successful, one MUST BE DISCIPLINED!

In 1 Corinthians 9:27, Paul says:

But I keep under my body, and bring it into subjection:
lest that by any means, when I have preached to others,
I myself should be a castaway.

Notice what Paul tells us here: **But I keep under my body, and bring it into subjection...** The "I" that Paul is talking about is the spirit man on the inside. "I" is the *real you.* "I" is the you that has been born again. Your body is not you. You are *not* flesh and blood.

Have you ever heard someone say, "Well, what do you expect? I am only flesh and blood. What do you want me to do, be an angel or something? I'm just flesh and blood."

You ARE NOT flesh and blood. You are a spirit! You *have* a flesh and blood body, but you are not flesh and blood. Flesh and blood is where *you* live. You are a spirit made in the image of God.

The great Apostle Paul said that he kept his body under and brought it into subjection. That tells me that the body is out of subjection, and if I do not bring my body in line, it will stay out of subjection.

Notice what Paul DID NOT say: He did not say, "I put my body under." If he had said that, he would only have to do it one time. But he said, *I KEEP my body under.*

The reason he had to keep it under was because it wanted to get out from under — the same way *your* body does. And if you do not keep that sucker under, it will get out from under and do something it is not supposed to do. Unfortunately, we hear about it getting out from under all the time in the ministry fraternity.

If you cannot discipline your body,
you will not discipline your spirit.

A minister of God has to be disciplined, and it starts with the flesh. If you cannot discipline your body, you will not discipline your spirit. You cannot! It is impossible! You cannot see your spirit, yet you are looking at your body every day, and it will get out of control if you let it. How are you going to control something you cannot even see?

You have a body that you are looking at all the time, you haul it around, you push it in and out of cars, you feed it, you are stuffing it, you pajama it, you suit it, you clothe it, you undershirt it, undershort it, you shave it, you spray cologne on it, you deodorize it, you bathe it; and sometimes it gets out of control — *while you are looking* at it every five minutes! How are you going to control your spirit, and you have not even seen it?

Paul said, *But I keep under my body and bring it screaming and hollering into subjection,* because screaming and hollering is what it will do. It does not want to conform. It is not subject to the laws of God. You have to bring it into submission and *keep* it there.

If you want to be successful, you have to discipline yourself. And it starts with your body. If God cannot trust you with the house you live in, why would he give you 5,000 members?

It costs something to be disciplined. It will make you scream sometimes. It will make you holler sometimes, because your body does not want to conform, but you have to make it conform and BRING it into subjection. Subjection to what? To the Word of God and to your own spirit. It does not work automatically, you have to stay with it all the time.

I like to eat. I love good food. I particularly enjoy ice cream. Sometimes I will get a craving for it just as they say some women who are pregnant have a craving for something.

Sometimes when I get that craving, just to let the devil know that I am in control, I will deny myself, and I will refuse to eat it. I tell my body, "I am in control — ME, the *spirit me*. The man on the inside is in control. Body, you do not control me!" No ice cream is going to have me crawling the walls at midnight trying to find a fix, like some preachers do with cigarettes.

I will say it again, because it bears repetition: A disciplined life is what you HAVE to have in order to be successful in your Christian life, as well as in the ministry!

#2
The Word of God Must Have
First Place in Your Life
(John 8:31,32)

John 8:31,32

Then said Jesus to those Jews which believed on him, If ye continue in my word, then are ye my disciples

indeed; And ye shall know the truth, and the truth shall make you free.

I had been reading this verse for days, and I thought I knew this simple verse of scripture. All of a sudden it dawned on me, that verse did not say *the truth will make you free.* It did not say that at all! That is what I always said, "The truth will make you free." No! It won't!

I will guarantee you that you will hardly find a Christian anywhere in the world who does not own a Bible. They have the truth, and yet they are just as whipped and defeated as any sinner.

They know where the truth is — it is in the Bible — but they are still defeated. Consequently, it must not be just **having** the truth alone that makes you free. But notice what Jesus says in this verse: **and ye shall KNOW the truth...** It is one thing to have the truth, but something else to *know* it.

As an example, a minister I heard about — and I am not trying to put him down — but here is the proof of this statement: The Bible says, **Thou shalt not commit adultery** (Ex. 20:14). The Bible says, **Flee fornication** (1 Cor. 6:18). Yet, this brother got someone pregnant who was not his wife. He is a minister. So, if the truth was going to make him free, he should have been free. But, it is one thing to have the truth and something else to *know* it. You may *have it,* but you *do not know it.* Because if you know it, and then not do it, what excuse can you give God?

Also, notice this, Jesus said, **If ye continue in my Word, then are ye my disciples indeed...** (John 8:31). If you just take that verse at face value, it appears that discipleship is based upon continuing in His Word. If that is true, then that would make salvation based on works, because continuing in the Word would mean doing what the Word says. Now that cannot be true, because *Ephesians 2:8,9* says, **For by grace are ye saved through faith; and that not of**

yourselves: it is the gift of God: Not of works, lest any man should boast.

What is Jesus talking about? Notice the word "indeed." If He had said, ... **then are ye my disciples** and put a period there, that would make a difference. But He said, "INDEED."

"Indeed" means there are some *real* disciples. They are what discipleship is all about. There are many Christians who are called disciples, who are born again, and who are learners, students, and followers, but they are not the "disciples *indeed*."

The ones INDEED are THE ONES WHO ARE WINNING! They are the ones who are doing something that is going to affect the enemy in a positive way — positive for the Body of Christ and negative for the enemy.

The Word of God HAS TO HAVE FIRST PLACE IN YOUR LIFE if you want to be successful in ministry.

#3
Prayer
(1 Corinthians 14:4)

The third thing necessary for a successful ministry is prayer. You cannot be successful in ministry without prayer. And I know there are many ministers who do not pray. I am a minister, and there was a time I did not pray.

First of all, I did not know *how* to pray, and secondly, I did not "have time" to pray because I was too involved doing things "for the Lord." How could I take time to pray? I was on this committee, I had to do this, I had to go there, I had the Ministers' Union over here, this meeting over there; I had too much to do to take time to pray.

You can get so involved in ministry, that you will never have time to pray. There are many, many preachers — if

they will be honest about it — who will have to admit they
do not pray.

...if you are not filled with the Holy Spirit,
you don't really know how to pray.

In fact, if you are not filled with the Holy Spirit, you
do not really know how to pray. The real prayer method
that will help you be successful is the method of praying
in the Spirit, and you cannot pray in the Spirit until you
are filled with the Holy Ghost and speak with other tongues.

1 Corinthians 14:4 says:

**He that speaketh in an unknown tongue edifieth
himself.**

The English words that really give the true meaning
of the word "edify" are the words *to charge*. For example,
you charge a battery. When the automobile battery in your
car runs down and you put it on a battery charger, what
you are doing is replenishing its electrical power.

When you pray with other tongues, that is what you
do to your spirit. You are putting your spirit on a
supernatural battery charger. Praying with tongues will keep
your spiritual battery completely charged at all times.

A minister should be "up" spiritually all the time.
There is no such thing as a "down" day. I used to have
blue Mondays, purple Tuesdays, orange Wednesdays,
chartreuse Thursdays, black Fridays, green Saturdays, and
brown Sundays! This should not be so in the man of God's
life who is walking in faith by the Word.

I have not had one down day in 20 years. When I found
out how to walk by the Word, I retired from down days!
I do not have them anymore. I have a lot of opportunities
to have them, but I decided to let the Word of God take
the place of down days. I attribute most of my overcoming

in this area to the fact that I spend much time praying in the Spirit.

Paul says, He that speaketh in an unknown tongue edifieth himself. As I stated before, the real you is a Spirit.

1 Corinthians 14:14,15

For if I pray in an unknown tongue, my spirit prayeth but my understanding is unfruitful (or literally *barren*).

What is it then? I will pray with the spirit, and I will pray with the understanding also (*or in addition to*): **I will sing with the spirit, and I will sing with the understanding also** (*or in addition to*).

I have what I call a "flip-flop" method of reading the Bible. What I do is flip it around and read what it does not say, and somehow, for me, it reinforces what it does say. For example, using this method, it would read, *For if I pray in an unknown tongue, my spirit prayeth; for if I do not pray in an unknown tongue, my spirit does not pray.* All that prays without my spirit is my mind or my soul. That is not good enough in this warfare we are involved in.

Praying without tongues has its time and place. When I pray over the food that is going into my body, I pray in English so everyone around me will be in agreement that the food is not going to harm us. In times such as this, you pray in English, but the true praying — whereby you *build yourself up on your most holy faith* as Jude 20 says — is praying with other tongues, praying in the Holy Spirit.

Every minister needs to spend time praying, and one should not be so busy doing things for God that he does not have time to talk to his Heavenly Father out of his own spirit.

In the book of Hebrews, the writer tells us that God is the Father of spirits. (Heb. 12:9.) It does not say He is the Father of flesh. He is the Father of spirits. He wants to talk to His spirit children, and He has given us a language by which we can talk to Him, which is praying — literally speaking — with other tongues.

I am not talking about the gift of tongues as recorded in First Corinthians 12, which operates with the companion gift of the interpretation of tongues. I am talking about the private, devotional tool that God has given to us by which to edify ourselves. And that is what you receive when you are filled with the Holy Spirit.

In summary, building up yourselves on your most holy faith, praying in the Holy Ghost is praying by the spirit — not your mind or your head. Any time you pray with your head, it is going to be predicated on your knowledge of the circumstances. I can only pray up to my knowledge of the situation, but the Holy Ghost knows every situation. If I will let Him give my spirit the information, my spirit will pray it out so that God can answer it back in the earth realm. That is the highest kind of prayer, and we need to edify ourselves. Ministers need to set time aside to pray in this manner.

> ...if I could give any one else an hour, I
> certainly should pray with tongues
> the same length of time.

I was a late sleeper. My wife could certainly tell you that. When that alarm clock would ring in the mornings, I would cry, literally cry — shed real tears! I just did not like getting up. I wanted to stay in bed a little bit longer. But I found out that if I was going to be a man of victory and a man of prayer, I was going to have to spend time in prayer. As a result, years ago, I started getting up at five o'clock in the morning. Some people get up earlier and some people get up later. But I began getting up at five a.m. to give my spirit an opportunity to exercise itself in the presence of the Father God.

I had decided to pray at least one hour with tongues each morning. I did not have a scripture stating how long one should pray, but I figured if I could give anyone else an hour, I certainly should pray with tongues the same length of time.

I sit and watch a television program for an hour, and that is not feeding anything. There is nothing wrong with watching television, but it is not really that beneficial. Therefore, I made up my mind to give God an hour each morning, praying to Him out of my own spirit.

God is no respecter of persons; therefore, there must be some deeper things involved that cannot easily be seen, which contribute to the success of larger, prosperous ministries — ministries such as Dr. Paul Yonggi Cho's ministry in Seoul, Korea.

As I stated previously, in the early years of my ministry, I was hardly praying at all. If I prayed an hour a year, it was miraculous. I did not know *how* to pray. All I said was, "Lord, have mercy. Have mercy, Lord. Bless me, Lord, and bless all the people in the hospitals; go to all the jails and bless everybody."

That is NOT praying! If you want to be successful, you are going to have to spend time praying in the Spirit, and that means with other tongues.

#4
Exercise
(1 Timothy 4:8)

If you want to be prosperous in ministry, you should do some physical exercise. Everyone should exercise. Too many preachers are out of shape. If the Lord did put His anointing on them, they would have heart failure. They can hardly walk up stairs without huffing and puffing because they are carrying all of that extra weight around.

1 Timothy 4:8

For bodily exercise profiteth LITTLE: but GODLINESS is profitable unto all things, having promise of the life that now is, and of that which is to come.

Glory to God! We do not need to do any physical exercise! The Bible says exercise **profiteth little.** But WAIT A MINUTE! Paul did not say it DID NOT profit. He said, it profiteth little. However, you OUGHT TO HAVE the LITTLE that it PROFITETH!!

Remember, we have this treasure in earthen vessels. (2 Cor. 4:7.) To the extent that the vessel functions, the Spirit of God will be able to flow through that body to minister to the needs of the people. If I am strapped in an iron lung, God is limited to that iron lung. God is limited by our limitations, because He does not do anything apart from the Body of Christ.

People ask me how I stay so slim. I stay slim by eating everything I want to eat and stuffing myself until I cannot see straight. NO!! That is *not* how! How do you expect someone to keep slim and trim? By watching what you eat and by consistently exercising properly. Generally speaking, as you get older, you cannot eat like you used to eat. You just can't do it!

Friend, there is primarily one thing that makes you gain weight, and that is *eating too much!* So do not lie to me and to God and to the devil and yourself. If you are getting bigger, it is because you are EATING too much!

Controlling one's weight by proper diet and proper exercise is a part of being successful. Keep in mind that your body is the temple of the Holy Ghost, and God works through that temple.

#5
Be an Example
(1 Peter 5:3)

As ministers of the Gospel, we have to be examples for those God has placed in our care. Being an example is what I attempt to do in everything I put my hands to. I am often criticized by those who do not understand my motives, but that is still my goal.

There may be many who do not understand what you are doing and they will think you are bragging. People often talk about me and Kenneth Hagin, saying, "There they go bragging again." They do not understand the difference between a good report and bragging.

God has to have examples, and you will not know what people are doing if they do not tell you. You cannot know simply by looking.

1 Peter 5:3

Neither as being lords over God's heritage, but being ensamples to the flock.

We, as pastors, are to be examples, or role models, to those we shepherd. If a minister is a role model in everything he does, the most probable result is that the congregation will be whatever he is. Because normally, whatever you find in the congregation, comes from the pulpit.

When Peter tells us to be examples to the flock, that means in every area — spiritually, mentally, physically, and in every other positive way. But most importantly, in the ways that people can see us, because they cannot see a person's heart. They can only see the exterior. Whatever the exterior is, that is what they will measure us by. This is the reason I share the way I do with my congregation.

Many times, people will not understand your motives and will begin to criticize you. Unfortunately, as soon as some people are criticized, they stop sharing, because they do not like the criticism. I don't either! However, I like the fact that people will be blessed more than I like the fact that I will not be criticized.

That gets into selfishness when you are more concerned about how you feel than about sharing with the people. So, I would rather share with the people and be criticized if it comes to that.

I have learned to take the attitude that what people say about me is irrelevant and immaterial. The only thing that counts with me is what God says about me. Whatever anyone else says, that is just *their opinion.*

After all, like the old saying goes, ''Beauty is in the eye of the beholder.'' I am not what I am because someone says I am. I am what I am because of what God says about me and because of how I agree with what God says about me.

We are examples, ministers of the Gospel. Our spouses are also examples.

#6
Endure Persecution and Criticism
(2 Timothy 3:10)

If you want to be successful in the ministry, prepare to be criticized. The only way that the devil can get to you is by getting to you! In other words, Satan cannot get to you unless you let him.

In 2 Timothy 3:10-12, Paul says:

But thou has fully known my doctrine, manner of life, purpose, faith, longsuffering, charity, patience,

Persecutions, afflictions, which came unto me at Antioch, at Iconium, at Lystra; what persecutions I endured: but out of them all the Lord delivered me.

Yea, and all that will live godly in Christ Jesus shall suffer persecution.

That word "suffer" means to contend with or to put up with. You will be persecuted, and the persecution will come in the form of criticism. That is a part of persecution. People will criticize you, and the devil will work through people to try and stop your witness and your testimony. That is how you can tell the growth pattern of a Christian.

If they get their feelings hurt, they are still babies. You have to get to the point where you say, "Hey, no problem!" This is not taking a negative attitude like saying "Well, *que sera, sera* — whatever will be will be."

We have this idea that persecution means they are going to burn you at the stake, put you in a vat of oil like they did John, or they are going to put pitch all over you and set you on fire like they did the Christians during the days of the Roman Emperor, Nero. That is not the only kind of persecution. Persecution can come from people talking and wagging their tongues about you. And it never stops!

I don't care how high up the ladder you get; I don't care how spiritual you become, people are going to talk about you. It is really not people, however, it is the devil. But the devil always has some person who is sitting around waiting to use his or her mouth to spew out a lot of garbage that is directed at the minister of God.

The person may not even know you, but he will criticize you. You know that has to be a fool talking. Why would you get upset about something he has said?

People will talk about you, write books about you, use your name in print, and get on television and talk about you *by name*! We, as Christians — particularly ministers — should not do that. Let God take care of folks. God does not need your help to take care of anybody. You have a full-time job taking care of yourself and the people under your care.

1 Peter 5:7 says,

Casting all your care on him; for (or because), **he careth for you.**

I was so glad when I found that out! That is where faith comes in. You cannot do that unless you learn how to operate by faith, because you are looking at the person who is standing right there criticizing you.

And if you do not know how to operate by faith, that can stop you.

But I have learned to cast all my care on the Lord. I do not have any cares. I have people who say to me, "With a big television ministry and a big church like that, I know you have a lot of burdens." I say, "That is *your* confession; that is not mine."

In fact, I almost feel guilty for getting paid sometimes. I really do, because it is that easy. There are no cares; there are no burdens. I have retired from them. If I cast all my cares on God, that means God has them, I don't. I'm free. How does a free man act? A free man has to start talking free, thinking free, and acting free.

In 1977, we ran out of room for Sunday morning church services and began having double services. It was not too long afterward that we went to triple services. We knew we needed more room. We sought another location.

It seemed to take forever to get the money. Finally, when we bought our present property, we knew we were going to build the FaithDome. It took three years to build it, starting from the time we broke ground until the time it was completed.

God is doing something, and He is giving
us the privilege to assist Him.

During that time, people would say, "What's going to
happen? Suppose the FaithDome doesn't get built?" I said,
"So what?! Suppose it doesn't get built? It doesn't get
built!" "Yes, but what are people going to think?" I would
answer, "What are people going to think? They are going
to think the FaithDome did not get built. That is what they
are going to think." "Yes, but aren't you going to be
embarrassed?" How could I be embarrassed? I am not
building any churches.

If I were going to build a FaithDome, I would have built
it in 1977 when we first ran out of room. I would not have
gone through all those years struggling with this thing. I
told the Lord a long time ago, "This is *your* church. I have
my job; I am an undershepherd under You."

The Bible does not say that we are workers FOR God.
The Bible says, *We are workers* **together WITH God.** (1 Cor.
3:9.) God is doing something, and He is giving us the
privilege to assist Him. You and I need to find our place
and take our jobs as assistants.

He does not want you to build a big church. He will
build the church. That is where many pastors make
mistakes. They want to do something for God. He does not
need us to do a thing for Him. He was God before we were
created, He is God now, and He will continue to be God
throughout eternity.

We have our responsibilities, but it is God Who is doing
the work. I told the Lord, "If you do not get the church
built, you are the One who is going to look bad, not me."

You cannot find anywhere in the Bible where it says, "My Fred Price will supply all my needs." No! God said *He* would!

I told myself that "If He does not supply the needs for the FaithDome, it won't get built, and it won't bother me in the least. I'm going to keep on teaching the Word. If God cannot get the people in, He does not need them. They are not my people. I cannot get anybody in. If there is no room, it is not my fault." I had to do my part, and I did all I knew how to do.

People kept telling me, "Oh, I know you must be under a lot of pressure." No, I wasn't! No, I don't operate under pressure — I don't deal with it. I don't have it. God said to cast all my care on Him and that is what I did. I cast all my care on Him.

Someone said to me once, "Man, I haven't slept for the last five nights. This thing has really got me." He did not realize that the Bible says, *God neither sleeps nor slumbers.* (Ps. 121:4.) Why in the world should I lose sleep? Why should *both* of us stay up all night?

Since God is going to be up anyway, I might as well go to sleep. There is no point in me staying awake. He can handle it better than I can anyway, and He does not need my help because He was God before I came into existence.

If you want to be successful, you are going to have to learn how to turn challenges and problem situations and people over to the Lord. People will drive you insane, and I don't just mean worldly people. I am talking about born-again, Spirit-filled, tongue-talking folks who will drive you to distraction if you allow them to.

If you don't want to be criticized,
you should find another career...

You will have many opportunities to become discouraged in the ministry. But do not give in to discouragement. I take the attitude, "What is there to be discouraged about in reality? God is still on the throne. I am still filled with the Holy Ghost; Jesus is still Lord, and He is still praying for me and interceding on my behalf. My name is still written in the Lamb's Book of Life. What in the world would I want to be discouraged about? I win. Any way I go, I win. I cannot lose. So, why be discouraged?"

Yes, you will be persecuted. You will be criticized. If you do not want to be criticized, you should find another career, because if you stay in ministry, you will be criticized. You will find out the more you do good, the more people will talk about you. *If you do not do anything,* nobody will criticize you.

Before I started getting into faith and telling folks about how to get healed, no one criticized me. They did not even know who I was. They did not know I existed. All of a sudden I became a big problem for the devil.

Before I got into faith and found out how to walk by the Word and found out who I was in Christ, I never received any criticism. I went 17 years and did not get criticized not even once, because I wasn't doing anything. I wasn't even fulfilling my assignment as an assistant to God. So, why should the devil go after me? Why would anyone shoot at a target that is not a threat to him? You do not waste ammunition on a non-essential target.

#7
Competition in the Ministry
(1 Corinthians 1:11-13)

Whether you realize it or not, there is competition in the ministry — ministers deliberately trying to be different from other ministers in order to attract "customers."

1 Corinthians 1:11-13

For it hath been declared unto me of you, my brethren, by them which are of the house of Chloe, that there are contentions among you.

Now this I say, that every one of you saith, I am of Paul; and I of Apollos; and I of Cephas; and I of Christ.

Is Christ divided? was Paul crucified for you? or were ye baptized in the name of Paul?

There is no room for competition among the brethren. There is no need for it. I always wanted to be a great singer. We all have our dreams. I like opera and I wanted to be a great tenor. I used to listen to some of the great operatic voices and I would think, "Why can't I sing like that?" But you know what I found out? I found out I do not have to be envious of anyone's abilities or talents, because I am unique. I am the only one like me in existence. We are all unique; consequently, we do not need to be in competition with anybody!

No one else has been given your assignment, and no one can fulfill it except you. You do not have to be in competition because no one else can do what you can do. No one can say it like you can. No one looks like you. No one thinks like you, so there is nothing to be in competition about.

Besides all that, there are millions of people in the United States who want to hear about the Lord. When preachers come to me and talk about their ministries not having enough people, some have made comments such as this: "I don't understand why the Lord is sending all those people over there to that church. We love the Lord. How come we don't have a large congregation like so and so's church?"

I say to them, "Wait a minute, Brother. Suppose next Sunday morning at 11 o'clock God sent 5,000 people to you. What are you going to do with them? You can only seat

40 people in your church; what can you possibly do with 5,000, or for that matter, 500? You are not equipped for that many people; you are not prepared. If 300 came forward in the invitation to receive Jesus, you wouldn't be able to minister to them. You don't have the personnel or anyone trained to do it.''

We do not need to compete with one another. All we need to do is what the Lord has told us to do. I thank God I am not trying to compete with anyone. I am just trying to do my job. I do not want to hear God say, ''Well, Fred, you are as good a preacher as so and so.'' I do not want to hear that. I want to hear my Heavenly Father say, **Well done, thou good and faithful servant** (Matt. 25:21).

We are all unique.

We are all unique. We all have our jobs to do. We were all sent to minister to a certain group of people, and that ought to thrill us.

Only certain people listen to me. There are people who would not cross the street to hear me. And I know this! I do not operate under any illusions. Everybody does not like my method of teaching; everyone is not ready for me; and I am not for everybody. I know it and I don't sweat it. I am believing God is going to send the people to me who will respond to my kind of personality, my kind of ministry, my kind of whatever it might be.

There are some ministers I cannot stand to listen to. There is no point in lying about it. I cannot stand to hear them speak. They would never minister to me. If I had to depend on them to bring me the message of salvation, I would go to hell. I cannot stand the whine in their voices. And I know there are people who feel the same way about me. Who cares, as long as they get saved.

It does not matter who they listen to as long as they are able to be ministered to by someone and hear the message of salvation. It does not have to be me, and it does not have to be you. God has someone to minister to everybody. All we have to do is to be faithful to what God calls us to do. Just BE FAITHFUL!

God has a way of working with us, but
sometimes we get ahead of His program.

One hears about Dr. Cho and his 500,000 members — the biggest church in the world. Can you imagine the challenge the man must have with 500,000 people? Everything that glitters is not gold. Friend, I can tell you this, he has the biggest challenges in the world with all those people. Think of how many members you have, and you have pains! Can you imagine 500,000 pains?

We can gain from one another, but we do not have to compete with each other, because no one else is like you or me. We do not have to get into doing something simply because someone else is doing it. I have to deal with this often within my own personality. You see someone with a program that is going good, and you have a tendency to want to emulate him. I have to catch myself and tell myself, "The Lord did not tell you to do that." You have to be single-minded and know what God has told *you* to do.

I have had people tell me, "Why don't you have a so and so program? Think what you could do with this great big church if you had that kind of program." People get upset with me because I do not have the kind of program they think I should have — such as feeding the poor. But God did not tell *me* to *develop* a program for feeding the poor, even though we participate in and financially support some of those kinds of programs.

I empathize with the poor, but I did not make them poor, and they do not have to be poor — at least not in America — if they would follow the Word of God. I can see being poor, perhaps in some part of Africa, way out in the bush country where civilization has not yet penetrated. Maybe there, one might be considered poor. But in metropolitan areas like most of the United States, if you are poor, it is because you have not taken steps to prevent poverty from overtaking you. If you are a Christian, you not only do not have to be poor, you *should not be* — because God is your Source!

There is no shortage of money. We have never had a 6 o'clock evening news commentator come on and say, "Well, I do not know what we are going to do. Things are really looking bad — we are running out of money."

Do not get intimidated and get into competition trying to do something because other ministers have successful programs. Maybe God told them to do what they are doing. If they are doing what God told them to do, they cannot help but be successful. If God did not tell them to do what they are doing, chances are success will not be theirs.

Do not conduct your ministry on a competitive basis trying to find out what everyone else is doing. There are a number of ministers who run to all kinds of church growth conferences. You cannot find out how to make a church grow by going to a conference.

I had a church growth conference some years ago. It was not really supposed to be a church growth meeting, but I did not know what to call it at the time.

I believed there was something God wanted me to do, but either I was not listening carefully enough and did not get the signals right, or I just did not know how to accomplish what the Lord wanted at the time. That is why when I started to have a second conference, I canceled it.

41

I said, "I am not going to do it! That is *not* what God told me to do."

God has a way of working with us, but sometimes we get ahead of His program. One day I was on vacation, reclining in the water, just out in the surf enjoying the water, and all of a sudden, the Lord showed me what to do and when it was time to do it. Fellowship of Inner-City Word of Faith Ministries (FICWFM) is the result of my following the Lord's leading.

No, you cannot go to a conference and find out how a church grows and make one grow by doing what someone else is doing. If you go to all the churches in the world that are growing, you will find they are all doing something different. They are all doing something different because the minister is different, and God told him to do it that way because that is what will work there — but it may not work anywhere else.

#8
Know the Difference Between
Bragging and a Good Report
(Mark 5:19,20)

In the fifth Chapter of Mark, we can read the story of Jesus going to Gadara where He found a naked man who was full of demons. Jesus cast them out of the man, and the demons asked Jesus not to send them out of the country. There was a herd of swine, and they asked to be sent into the swine. And when the demons entered into the pigs, they ran off a cliff and were drowned in the water below. (Even pigs have enough sense not to be demon possessed!)

Afterwards, the man was clothed and found to be in his right mind. When it was all over, the people of the town came and were afraid of Jesus. They did not understand what had happened and they asked Him to leave their vicinity. As He was about to depart, the man asked Jesus if he could go with Him. In Mark 5:19,20, it states:

> **Howbeit Jesus suffered him not** (or in other words, permitted him not), **but saith unto him, Go home to thy friends, and tell them how great things the Lord hath done for thee, and hath had compassion on thee.**
>
> **And he departed, and began to publish in Decapolis how great things Jesus had done for him: and all men did marvel.**

The next time Jesus came to that area, the folks were waiting for him as a result of that man's testimony. You have to know the DIFFERENCE BETWEEN BRAGGING and GIVING A GOOD REPORT and telling how great things the Lord has done for you.

The Lord has directed me in my spirit to share certain things. And sometimes, to be frank with you, I am a bit embarrassed when I tell some of the things that I tell. I really feel uneasy on the inside, but I know the Lord is directing me to do it because it will minister to certain people.

It may not minister to everyone, but God wants me to share it because you cannot see what is going on on the inside. So I tell people about certain things in order for them to know about the workings of God. And I relate the things they cannot see to the things they can see — the things one can see are usually the results of things one cannot see. (For example, a standing field of corn that is ready to be harvested is the result of seed sown that at one time could not be seen above ground!)

Therefore, if I relate a certain incident, it is a result of a seed that was planted some time back. If I do not tell them, they will not know what has been accomplished. But if I say, "This is what the Lord has done," they can be encouraged and inspired because God is no respecter of persons.

43

That is the reason I tell so many personal things, and many people criticize me for doing so. But I have learned to go above and beyond all that so that people can be helped to apply the Word of God uncompromisingly to their lives.

When I first found out about divine healing, I was so excited. Someone pointed me to it, and I saw it in the Word. I really got elated. I said, "Oh, this is wonderful! I can be healed!" And I sat around waiting for the devil to put something on me so I could take my new-found faith and knowledge and knock it in the head! I was ready for a fight!

I thought that was God's best, until one day I heard a man say, "I haven't been sick in 35 years." I said, "WHAT?" All of a sudden it dawned on me — divine healing was not God's best, divine health was!

Why get sick and have to be healed? Why not stay well and not have a need to be healed? If I had not heard that testimony, perhaps I would still be going around today waiting for the devil to put something on me. Thank God I found out that I do not have to be sick!

Thank God you can be healed, but it is better to walk in divine health and never need to be healed. How would I have known that if someone had not shared that with me? People accused that man of bragging. No! He was not bragging. He was just telling what great things the Lord had done. IT'S CALLED A TESTIMONY!!

If you want to be successful in ministry, you need to know the difference between the two! If you do not, you can short-circuit your faith by thinking you are doing things in your own strength instead of giving glory where it belongs — to the Lord!

#9
Take Time With Your Spouse and Your Children
(Mark 6:30-31)

This may hit you in the face, so put your seat belt on!

Mark 6:30,31 says:

> And the apostles gathered themselves together unto Jesus, and told him all things, both what they had done, and what they had taught.
>
> And he said unto them, Come ye yourselves apart into a desert place, and rest a while: for there were many coming and going, and they had no leisure so much as to eat.

That is the way ministry can be. Ministers are denying their spouses and families vacation time away from the church and time away from the ministry. These ministers have the wrong idea. They think they are going to save everyone by themselves. That is *ego* going somewhere to happen. Read the verses again:

> And the apostles gathered themselves together unto Jesus, and told him all things, both what they had done, and what they had taught.
>
> And he said unto them, COME YE YOURSELVES APART INTO A DESERT PLACE (that is away from the church), AND REST A WHILE.

You need to take your vacations, and you need to take your family somewhere. That church or ministry will run without you. I know it is hard to conceive that the people, or that the ministry, or that God can get *anything* done *without you*! I know it is very difficult for you to accept that.

Some ministers have church telephones in their private homes that are ringing all day and all night long. You think you are God? You have a telephone, a line from the church into your house, so that people can get you 24-hours a day. You are trying to save the world, and your own family is going to pieces. Your children are running wild. You have no time for your spouse, because you have to be down at the church all the time. You had better learn how to take time off and go on your vacations!

45

The first thing I put on my calendar every year is my vacations. If I don't I would never get one — never in life! There is something to do all the time; 24-hours a day someone needs help. I cannot solve all their problems.

God never said that Fred Price was the need-provider. The Word says **My God shall supply . . .** (Phil. 4:19). It does not say Fred Price will supply. You have to turn people over to God.

Yes, you have a responsibility to your flock, but Jesus never said anything about holding folks in your arms. He said, **Feed my sheep** and **feed my lambs.** That is all He said to do. And you are trying to hold up people and carry the whole burden of your congregation. You end up being God for them, then you get them hooked on you. And when you do get out of pocket, out of reach, they can't function. They are out of it, because their dependence has always been on you. You do all their praying; you do all their interceding; you are the ears that always listen to their problems. Let them talk to *God; He* is the problem-solver.

You cannot always know everyone in your church. If you want to know everyone by name in your church, then prepare to have a small church — very small!

There is a price to pay to do the will of God. And that price is that you are going to have to end up seeing people as people that you can help just so much. The rest is up to them and the Lord.

Learn how to rest. When I have a day off, I take the telephone off the hook. I unplug it. If I go to hotels, I unplug the phones. If I do not have the kind of phone in the room that you can unplug, I take the receiver off the hook. Someone is always calling about something. You will be up all day and all night, so learn how to take some time off with your spouse. That is why God gave you a helpmeet — to be your companion and helper.

#10
Feed the Flock
(1 Peter 5:2)

There are many scriptures to support teaching the Word to your people. However, I am only going to share one verse.

1 Peter 5:2

Feed the flock of God which is among you, taking the oversight thereof, not by constraint, but willingly; not for filthy lucre, but of a ready mind.

Notice what it does *not* say. It does not say to "entertain" them. It says **feed** them. And really, the only thing that feeds people is teaching. Christians do not need preaching. They might — like little babies — want to hold on to a pacifier, which is usually what emotional preaching is. Have you ever seen a child five years old with a pacifier in his mouth? That is a tragic sight, but I have seen it.

Some spiritual babies will try to hold on to you, but you should keep teaching them and pointing them to the Word. You are *not* helping them with emotional sermons that keep them in bondage and tied to the minister.

Awhile back, a popular Black magazine did an article on the 10 greatest Black preachers in America. Some of my members came to me very upset, saying: "Your name wasn't in there! Why wasn't your name present?" I said, "I am not a preacher. The magazine said the 'greatest preachers,' and if you listen to those men, they are great preachers."

There is a difference between preaching and teaching. Preaching is more inspirational, where teaching is more informational. Sinners need preaching to inspire them to get saved. Christians need teaching to know what to do with their salvation.

We got caught up in emotional preaching when I was in a certain denominational church, trying to whoop, making a certain sound, and all of that. It was games and entertainment. We were not feeding the people, nor giving them anything to live on. We were only giving them that sweet pill of emotion week by week.

We have a great responsibility as ministers of the Gospel. Jesus said to Peter, **Feed my sheep** and **feed my lambs.** Preaching is for sinners, teaching is for Christians. Sinners need to be inspired to get saved; Christians should not need any inspiration. They should be their own inspiration if they are taught properly in the Word.

Some people have said we do not have a long enough period of time for singing during our service. Some folks have come and wanted to sing for 25, 35, 40 minutes — and *standing* all that time! My feet would be killing me! I couldn't even keep my mind on the Lord for thinking about how my feet were hurting.

Some churches have people standing a long time singing praise songs because they think they have to "work up" something. I come to church worked up. I *stay* worked up. I only have *one* speed, and that's GO! And it is on GO! all the time. I do not have to turn it down or turn it up. I am inspired all the time through the Word and my love for the Lord.

I have heard people say, "Well, bless God, you have to get up every morning and put on the armor (as indicated in Eph. 6:11). Don't go out of the house without your armor!"

I have never found any scripture in the Bible where God ever said to take the armor off. It only says *put it on.* Once on, it *never* comes off! You sleep in it, eat in it, and do everything else in it.

The same thing goes for inspiration; there is no greater inspiration (or rather there *should not be*) for the Christian than the Word of God. If you are a full-fledged, bona fide minister of the Gospel, filled with the Spirit, and you still need to be inspired, you may want to check your Word level.

In summary, do what God has called you to do; do what He has anointed you to do; do what He has given you a vision to do. Continually speak His Word. Meditate and DO the Word. Walk by faith — by the Word — and be motivated by love. Your ministry will produce fruitful results and you shall have good success.

APPENDIX

During Dr. Frederick K.C. Price's ministry travels to conferences, crusades, luncheons, and other ministerial gatherings, he is often asked questions about his successful ministry. Those questions run the gamut from queries about faith, to Biblical questions, to questions about his very personal life. Therefore, on the following pages, we have compiled the most frequently asked questions from his meetings throughout the years.

We believe this questions and answers section will be most informative and helpful in sorting out particular answers to questions ministers may have concerning their own ministry.

In fact, because of the detailed, in-depth answers provided, we believe the reader will be ministered to in a very special way. Rather than simple, pat, quick answers to questions, Dr. Price has provided Bible-based answers in addition to common-sense answers to some oftentimes pressing and interesting questions.

As a result, what this section becomes is another forum for teaching godly principles. It is really a ONE-ON-ONE CONVERSATION with DR. PRICE, rather than mere questions and answers.

Practical Suggestions for Successful Ministry

Questions and Answers — One-on-One With Fred Price

1. *Question:*

What would you suggest for a young man whose ministry is really starting to take off, as far as preparing himself more to reap the benefits of the ministry?

Dr. Price:

Whatever ministry God has called you to do, the basic element is that you first prepare yourself *spiritually;* meaning you should build yourself up in the Spirit. You should pray in the Spirit, so that your spiritual battery is up and fully activated at all times.

You should also STUDY THE WORD. That is an ongoing process until either Jesus comes back or until you leave this physical realm. Then, simply be faithful in whatever God has called you to do. And only you know what God has called you to do. As each opportunity arises, take advantage of it and give it all you have. Keep doing it — be FAITHFUL and CONSISTENT.

2. *Question:*

How much time do you spend confessing and praying for humanity, praying for the congregation, preparing for study and also physically exercising?

Dr. Price:

Understand that time, *per se,* is not the key. In other words, if I pray 24 hours every other day, that is great, but I do not think prayer is *automatically* going to make you successful.

However, you do need to set some standards for yourself. With the standards I have set for myself, I normally pray six days out of seven. I do not pray on Sunday, because I am working on Sunday, and if I am not ready for Sunday, forget it anyway. I pray Monday through Saturday, and I am ready for Sunday.

The rule I made for myself for my daily devotion is this: I pray one hour in tongues, then it usually takes me about 25 to 30 minutes to pray the rest of the things I have to pray about in English — such as the church and people, etc. And it does not take that long to do that.

That is my spiritual exercise; it is what I decided to do FOR ME. I am not saying there is some magic in that. It is just what I decided to do for myself personally. I started out with 15 minutes in the Spirit, then 20, then 45, and now I pray for an hour.

I also have a certain amount of Scripture I read. I do not have a great deal of time now to study like I used to. It was good for me to study hour after hour when I had the time and did not have many demands on my time. But because I did spend all the time that I did — reading, studying, and programming the Word into me like you program a computer — I can afford now to study the Word on a piecemeal basis, because it adds to the knowledge I have already studied.

Even so, there is a certain amount of Scripture I read — five chapters Monday through Friday, and 10 chapters on Saturday. Since I have to work on Sunday, I do not pray or read then.

That is what I call my minimum daily requirement. Any other time I have that I can give to prayer, study, or both those things, I do it, but that is "catch as catch can," depending upon the demands on my time.

As for exercise, I believe that I have this treasure in an earthen vessel. The Bible says bodily exercise profiteth little, but I believe if it profits ANY, we ought to have the little it profits. As long as the vessel is good, sound, and hardy, it makes it much easier for the treasure to flow out of it. My wife and I are involved in an exercise program and we exercise three times a week, Monday, Wednesday and Friday. We do this to keep our muscles toned, and our heartbeat, respiration and blood circulation going, and our bodies limber and trim.

3. *Question:*

When your church was growing, did you have some kind of hours where you would say, "This is the only time

I am open to ministry''? How do you go about teaching people not to call the pastor for everything from the toilet being busted to whatever, without appearing to be a snob, and without hurting people's feelings?

Dr. Price:

That is a very loaded question, but a very important one. One of the things you have to learn early in your ministry is to set some rules for yourself. YOU have to set them, because the people will not set them, and God will not set them. Sometimes Satan will try to work you into a state of condemnation by making you think you do not work for the people if you do not do certain things. If you yield to that thought, you end up running yourself ragged, and you still do not answer all their questions or solve all their problems.

Once I found out what the Word of God really said, and how to operate in it, I endeavored to *teach it* to the people, because the cure for their problems *is* the teaching of the Word. If you make that paramount and pre-eminent in the ministry, that will cut down on many things.

Again, we have this treasure in earthen vessels. If the vessel is ''shot to pot,'' the anointing cannot go anywhere. I do not care how much anointing you have. The ANOINTING WILL KILL THE VESSEL. You have to get your rest, or you will not have anything to give to the people. That means you cannot waste everything on one person. You could minister to a group of 50 people better than you could to just one — but there will be times when you have to deal with *one.*

Until such time as you are in full-time ministry, or part-time, to the point that you are in the church office three or four hours a day, and have a secretary who can screen your calls, you may have to set a certain time in the evening, and tell your congregation to call you between such and such a time. So, you set the time, and then have them understand what you have done. Instruct them. You may have to do it over and over until they learn that. When they continue calling at a time they are not supposed to call, and cannot get you, then they will get the hint. NEVER LET SATAN PUT YOU IN BONDAGE ABOUT THIS. He will try to get you into a guilt trip about it, and tell you, "Well, you really don't care about the people. Why are you so cold? If you really loved the people, you would be available all the time." That is the biggest lie ever told. What are you giving to the people, anyway, except what you get from the Father? If you do not have any time to get anything from the Father, you will soon be drained, and the devil will see to it that there are people there for the purpose of draining you.

YOU NEED TIME TO BE ALONE and take care of what you have to do to keep in shape. Even Jesus did that. There were times He separated Himself from the disciples for just that reason.

4. Question:

I believe one of the major things I have gathered is that you believe an evangelist, preacher or pastor should be disciplined; they should have balance in their lives, and they should set godly examples.

What do you do with your spare time when you leave the church each day? My wife and I have a real burden on our hearts to do something for Jesus, but we really do not know what to do as far as entertainment. And we want to be a good example. Other than spend time in the Word, what do you do to entertain yourself and to relieve yourself of the burdens and anxieties of the day?

Dr. Price:

First of all, I have no burdens or anxieties of the day. That does not mean they do not make themselves available to me, but I always say, "Passez vous," which means, "Pass on by!"

When I learned 1 Peter 5:7, that was the end of my ever having any more cares, worries, or problems. I cast my care upon the Lord. I have opportunities to be worried and frustrated, but I have better sense than that. I am a worker together with God. He is not a worker together with me. And He is big enough to handle any "problem" that arises. When I walk away from my office at the end of the day, I leave that "problem" there.

As far as how to spend your own time, that depends on what you want and like to do. You can read, go swimming, go bowling — it is not something "cut and dried." Of course, you should have enough sense to know you cannot go gambling, drinking, and carousing. That would be a bad testimony. But find whatever gives you pleasure within the parameters of a godly life, and do that. For each person, it is something different, but you need some leisure time.

5. *Question:*

Undoubtedly, people come into your ministry from denominational churches. What method do you use, if any, to inform those other churches that members have come your way, in order to maintain an ethical and moral relationship and good standing in your city?

Dr. Price:

When you talk about ethical, moral relationships and good standing in your city, I do not have it, anyway. Preachers criticize me, shoot me down, lie about me, preach sermons about me, castigate me, and everything else, so I couldn't care less about what they think.

If I went to someone's house, knocked on the door, and told the person to join Crenshaw Christian Center, that would be, as far as I am concerned, immoral and unethical. I do not do that. All I do is preach the Word. I believe the people will come, and I thank the Lord in advance for sending them.

Besides that, ALL the people belong to Jesus. They do not belong to the church on the corner, or to Crenshaw Christian Center.

THEY BELONG TO JESUS CHRIST. They are HIS sheep. *He* died for them. *He* redeemed them, and *He* is their *Head.* Wherever they go to church is irrelevant, other than the fact they are being fed. God is not impressed with the name over anyone's door. If the people leave one church and go to another, that is between them and the Lord.

6. *Question:*

We have a real tendency in the church for people to float around from church to church. On one hand we hear, ''Go where you get fed,'' and on the other hand, even if the Apostle Paul is preaching across town, they are to ''be in your own church.''

What is the importance of church membership, or what statement do you make to teach them the importance of church membership?

Dr. Price:

The whole idea of the corporate syndrome is to gather the sheep and the lambs together in a sheepfold. And a sheepfold is EXACTLY what the local church is, so the sheep can be fed and ministered to. The whole idea is, if you are being fed and ministered to at a local church, that is where you should go.

The Word indicates, and I will occasionally mention this to the congregation — that we should not forsake the assembling of ourselves together. That lets us know that we are to look out for one another.

However, if we have a certain meeting that comes to town, such as Kenneth Copeland's or Kenneth Hagin's ministry, and it is close enough to our church that I know the majority of the congregation would be able to very conveniently attend, I encourage it. For example, if the meeting is on a Tuesday night when I have my Bible study at the church — I will cancel my class and encourage the people to attend the other meeting, simply because that ministry comes to our area only occasionally.

The people can hear me every week. Besides, the visiting ministry may be a facet of the Body of Christ that is somewhat different from my ministry, and it may be something the people should be exposed to. So I will say, "All the Bible studies are canceled for the first three nights of the week, and I encourage you and expect you to go over there to the such and such meeting, if it is close enough."

On the other hand, if the meeting is so far away that I know 90 percent of the people will not go, we will go ahead and have our own services. We have nine Bible studies at Crenshaw Christian Center during the week, in addition to our Sunday morning service, so there is no real need for someone to go somewhere else if he or she simply wants to be fed the Word.

7. Question:

How do you handle situations when a person from another church comes to your church; you know the person's pastor and are together with him, but you do not want to be a divider? You do not want to steal the other pastor's sheep, but you want to see their needs met. Does that put you in a precarious situation?

Dr. Price:

No, it does not. Again, one of the things you have to learn early on is that ALL THE SHEEP BELONG TO JESUS. People have left my church and gone to churches of pastors I know, pastors who are feeding their congregations on the

Word. I do not care where they go, as long as they are getting the Word.

What you should do is MINISTER THE TRUTH to them when they come to you. Do not think about where they come from. You minister life to them. They came to you and asked for life. GIVE IT TO THEM. Leave the rest to the Lord, and do not let Satan intimidate you.

8. *Question:*

Recently the Lord called me to the ministry, and since that time, He has accelerated the doors being opened for me to minister the Word of God. I desire that my wife be with me when it is feasible, but I also have three young sons who have to be taken care of. I have always noticed, even in other cities and other states, your wife is always with you, and you also have a family.

How do you manage your time in terms of your priorities for your family and your ministry? And what sacrifice, if any, has it had upon your kids when your wife goes along with you?

Dr. Price:

When I got to the point of being in a traveling ministry, our two older daughters were of a pretty responsible age. When I first began traveling, however, I traveled alone, and it got lonely out there. I wanted my wife to come along with me, and it worked out to where she could accompany me, and we could get one of the church members to come and stay with the kids.

At the time, our youngest daughter was still a little too young for us to leave, but we found that the two older girls could manage pretty well with her, as long as they had supervision.

In fact, one time when we returned home, they told us, "We don't like the way so-and-so cooks. We like the way Mama cooks better, so we want to learn to cook the way she does, and to stay by ourselves next time." Our girls are very independent, and we have taught them to be that way.

We did become concerned when my wife became pregnant with little Fred, because you have to take care of a baby. However, the Lord worked it out. He gave us a person to live with us and take care of little Fred until he was pre-school age. Now, since all three of our daughters are married and have moved out, he stays with one of the members of the church when we are away, so he can continue going to school while we are gone.

I would say that when you are first starting out and you have little children, your wife has to be there with the kids. That is one of the sacrifices you will have to make in terms of growing in the ministry, because the first priority is to take care of the children. When they get big enough to be self-sufficient, and perhaps need just a little supervision, then you can take your wife with you.

9. Question:

My husband is a minister, and I am a stockbroker. Do you have a word of advice for when there are two professions in a household? Also, is it scripturally bad to have two professions in a household?

Dr. Price:

If God calls you to be an apostle, a prophet, an evangelist, a pastor or teacher, you should be that. If God has not called you, then you can be whatever you want to be, whatever your abilities, talents, and likes are, provided it is consistent with a godly life. God does not care where you work, because He can use you wherever you are.

When there are two professions in a family, there has to be *agreement* by the two parties involved that there will be two professions. Otherwise, you will have problems. If your husband objects to your being what you want to be, the two of you will have to reconcile it.

There is nothing wrong with the persons in the marriage being in different professions. They can complement one another. You can still pray for him, and you can still assist him when you are not busy, like on Saturdays and evenings, depending on your workload. If you are too busy all the time to help him, you are working too hard. What is most important, however — and what will determine whether it works or not — is that you two are in agreement, one way or another.

10. *Question:*

For a minister who is called of God, who is supposed to give himself totally to his calling, and to meditate upon what God has given him, what practical advice can you give in the area of meditation for the minister? As I understand from the Word of God, he cannot be a success unless he does this.

Dr. Price:

That gets into the area of a person's personal habits and lifestyle. It also has to do with what a person is involved in. Everyone is *different*. Some people are more prone to deeper thinking, contemplation, meditation. Other men are more energetic.

What you need to do is find out what works best for you, then *do it!* If it is standing on your head wiggling your toes five times a day, fine, go ahead. There are some things we can draw from other ministers, but we have to understand the time frame in which they lived, where they were, and what they were involved in. You may read about a minister praying in tongues five hours each day, and that is great, but you may not have five hours each day in which to pray in tongues. You may get more benefit out of something else, such as reading the Word.

We ought to pray and study the Word, but there is nothing in the Word that tells us how long to do those things each day. It does not tell us to read 99 chapters a day, pray 3-1/2 hours in tongues and two hours in my native language to qualify for my degree in spirituality. How much time you spend on those things depends on what else you have to do throughout the day.

11. *Question:*

What is your advice to a young pastor whose ministry is developing and who is contemplating marriage?
Dr. Price:

I would advise you to get married. Be sure that you have the mind of the Lord on the subject, and that you are marrying the right woman, but go with it. Especially if you are a pastor, you need to be married. It will "close a lot of doors" for you. You are human.

Everyone who comes to church is not coming for the Word. Some of the most beautiful women in the world come to Crenshaw Christian Center. There are many people, men and women, married and unmarried, who are looking for a bed partner. People are people, and you will not have any better success than the churches written about in the Bible. The people at the church in Corinth were Spiritfilled, and all the gifts of the Spirit worked there, yet there was a man there who was sleeping with his father's wife!

You will be in better shape if you are married, but do not run out and get married just for that reason. If you are in love, and want a helpmeet and a family, get married. However, the person you want for your wife needs to know where you are going, and she has to be in full agreement with it.

I do not care how beautiful she is, how finely formed her physique is, or how much she turns you on, if she is not 100 percent with the ministry of Jesus, do not marry her. If you are a tongue-talker, she had better be. If you believe in healing, she had better believe also, or you will have problems.

It goes back to 2 Corinthians 6:14: **Be ye not unequally yoked together with unbelievers....** Most of the time, this scripture is used for the subject of Christians marrying non-Christians, but it is just as valid concerning what two Christians believe. If one spouse believes in divine healing, and the other one does not, you are unequally yoked, even if you are both Christians.

12. *Question:*

How do you find time to satisfy your family's needs — or do you find enough time?

Dr. Price:

I am a very disciplined person, and I found out a long time ago that I cannot do all my life's work in one straight shot. Therefore, I allocate certain times that I hold inviolate, and I do not let anything interfere with that time.

For example, I take Mondays off, because Sunday is my heavy day, and I am exhausted after Sunday. On Mondays, my wife and I usually spend the time together, and I do not let anything interfere with that. I will not talk to anybody on Monday other than my family, and I do not take any calls. If necessary, I take the phone off the hook so that we can eat. Of course, we also have an unlisted number. We had to get that when we went on television.

We also take vacations together. We take part of my vacation in the springtime, in the summer, and part of it in the winter. For the summer vacation, we usually plan six months in advance to go somewhere, and we bring little Fred with us. For the winter vacation, I usually take the last three weeks of the year off. Little Fred is out of school, so I just spend the time around the house with the wife and kids.

13. *Question:*

I am from Jackson, Mississippi, and the reason I mention that is because of the question I have to ask. We have more Blacks in Mississippi than in any other state, and I catch myself continually feeling internal pressures because of saying, "I want to help the Blacks." It just cost me 16 years in my denomination; I moved out. Should I be feeling these internal pressures about stating, "I want to help the Blacks," even to the Blacks? The Civil War is over for me, but for a lot of people, it is not.

Dr. Price:

I got it, Brother, and I appreciate it. All you have to do is physically and spiritually be available. Preach the Word, pray, and ask the Lord to send the people to you. The Holy Spirit knows the people who are hungry. He knows what you will and will not do. Trust the Spirit of God to bring the people to you.

They will see your caring in your ministry. They will see it in the Word you minister. You do not have to say it. You do not have to convince them with your words. Convince them by your actions, by your being available, by your treating them as equals when you have the opportunity, and by giving them the uncompromised and unvarnished Word of God — and they will know. They will experience your spirit.

You should not feel guilty about it, or feel any pressures about it. You commit to the Lord, and say, "Lord, you know these people need so-and-so. I am available. If you can use me as a channel, I am available." Forget it after that, and go ahead and minister the Word. Let the chips fall where they may, and let the Spirit of God bring the people to you. He will bring them. When you minister that Word to them, your heart will be communicated through that Word, and they will know that you truly love them.

You do not have to say, "Some of my best friends are Black," for Black people to know you are sincere. Your actions, the way you relate to them on a personal level, and what you give them in the Word will let them know you are a real man of God.

14. *Question:*

In regards to the operation of the gifts of the Spirit, and doing things decently and in order, so that Sister Big Mouth does not go and "do her thing," what do you do as far as keeping that decently and in order — especially in a service with so many people?

Dr. Price:

Right from the beginning, I ran a very tight ship. We have taught people how to conduct themselves in the church when gifts of the Spirit manifest. As a result, we have had very few situations where anything got out of hand.

Basically, we have operation of the gifts of divers kinds of tongues, interpretation of tongues, and prophecy on a regular basis. The people are instructed that everything is done decently and in order. No one interrupts anyone else. If someone speaks out in tongues, it is interpreted. Whoever the worship leader is, he controls the situation. He has been trained and instructed, and he knows what to do.

If someone gets out of order, we just tell him to stop. If that person does not stop, I tell the ushers to come out quickly. They are instructed to go, physically pick up that person, if necessary, and carry him out instantly. I have had to do that only a couple of times. So, there is good order, and yet, there is freedom — but it is freedom within order.

As large as we are, we have the gifts of the Spirit operating regularly. We encourage them, we pray for them, we desire them, we covet that they would operate; consequently, we allow them to function. We just simply maintain order.

Many times, we have people who will get up and speak, and I know in my spirit that they are just talking out of their prayer language. There is no anointing on it. Therefore, we use a rule based on 1 Corinthians 14:27, where it says, **If any man speak in an unknown tongue, let it be by two, or at the most by three, and that by course; and let one interpret.** When we get our complement of three tongues and interpretations, we cut it off. We may have some prophecy in English after the cutoff, but that is it.

As long as whatever a person says in an interpretation or prophecy is consistent with the Word of God, even if there is no anointing in it, there is always benefit from the Word of God. It may not carry the inspiration that it would if it were anointed to be a prophetic utterance — to edify, exhort, and comfort — but it is still the Word of God. When you get to the utterance that just turns the place out and lifts you up, it is worth the wait.

Do not be afraid to maintain order. As soon as the devil knows he cannot pull anything off in your congregation, and as people start saying, "Don't mess up in there. They will carry you out," it will have a sobering affect on people who come to your church, in a beneficial sense. Any time anyone interrupts anything else going on in the service, that person is totally out of order. He should be squelched instantly, because what he is saying is not of the Holy Spirit.

15. *Question:*

Concerning the fellowship of believers in a church the size of yours, if there is no time for the people to get together other than for the large services, how do they fellowship? With our church, we have started what we call "house churches," meetings in homes where we have men raised up by the Lord from the congregation to be pastors to the smaller groups. What type of fellowship do you see in a program like that, especially in churches the size of yours?

Dr. Price:

We do have fellowship in that we have a Women's Fellowship, a Men's Fellowship, etc. The Women's Fellowship consists of every woman of the church. When she joins the church, she automatically becomes a member of that group. They meet monthly and have seminars, workshops, fellowship, and luncheons. Once a year, they have a Women's Retreat, where it is just the women together, at which time they have an opportunity to interact.

The Men's Fellowship follows a similar format, and so does the Singles' Fellowship. So there is opportunity for members to have intimate and interpersonal interaction with one another.

As for home meetings — this is just my own observation, and my own way of doing things — I discourage anything done in home meetings. I am not telling you not to have them, because the Spirit of God may tell you to do that, and God forbid that I should countermand the direction of the Spirit of God. However, I have found in our experience that when people get together in home gatherings, many times what are called "seducing spirits" get in. People begin "prophesying" to each other about whom they should marry and things like that. We are aware of some terrible experiences, which have occurred — not in our church, but in other situations.

That does not mean people in our church cannot have home meetings. I have no control over what someone does once he or she leaves the premises of Crenshaw Christian Center. However, I let members know that the church does not sanction or encourage them to have home meetings. If they do anything at home, it is between them and the Lord. They cannot blame the church for what may happen in a home meeting, and they cannot bring the church's name down as a result of what may happen. They are not meeting as a bona fide representative of Crenshaw Christian Center, because we have no way of controlling it.

16. *Question:*

How did you know your assistant pastors were going to teach what you teach, or walk in agreement with what you teach?

Dr. Price:

Every minister I have on my staff came directly out of my ministry. They grew up under the Word and what I teach from it, and they know the direction God is directing me in. As a result, they know the direction the church is going, and are in agreement with it. Also, I watch a person very closely for a while before I ask him to be a part of our team.

Sometimes people change on you in midstream, but at least initially, they know the direction I am going in, what I will tolerate, and what I will not tolerate. Then, of course, we have pastors' staff meetings every week, where we kick around ideas, and answer questions that arise. This way we can be in agreement and say the same thing in all of our classes.

I am not going to say, "Jesus is coming before the Tribulation," then have one assistant pastor say, "Jesus is coming in the middle of the Tribulation," and another assistant pastor say, "Jesus is coming at the end of the Tribulation." We all say the same thing or nothing at all, so the people will not be confused.

17. *Question:*

How do you handle the job responsibility for your assistant pastors? Do you have something you write out which says, "You do this task this week"? Or do you have a lot of overlap?

Dr. Price:

When I hire a man to be an assistant pastor — and I have learned this from experience — he and I sign a written job description or agreement. It spells out his job title, a detailed job description, his salary, and the benefits that will accrue. It also spells out other requirements I expect him to meet. For example, every pastor on my staff is to attend the Men's Fellowship meetings. That is a requirement. I explain what is on the agreement very carefully to the person, then he signs it, I sign it, and I keep a copy of it on file.

When I have hired women to come on the pastoral staff, they have signed a similar agreement. The only difference between what they sign and what the men sign is that the women's job titles have not been "pastor." That is because I have not yet found any scripture in the New Testament that I can live with which justifies a woman as a pastor. I do not mean to offend anyone with that statement. If God tells a woman to pastor a church, I am not going to say He did not say it. All I will say is, she will not work at Crenshaw Christian Center with the job title of "pastor."

The women I have hired have been given the job title, "Special Ministries." They have not been called pastors. However, they have pastoral duties, like when Paul told Timothy to do the work of an evangelist. Timothy was a pastor, but he did the work of an evangelist. So, even though he did not have the title, he did the same job as someone with the title "evangelist," and he got the same credit as well.

Each of the people on my pastoral staff has a job assignment. There are some general things we all do, but each of the assistants is accountable for a specific assignment. That assignment is spelled out very clearly, and they know their job duties.

18. *Question:*

How do you feel about women who have been called to the ministry?

Dr. Price:

If God did not want women in the ministry, He would not sanction their ministries by anointing them, and there would not be any results in them. That would soon discourage women from wanting to be in the ministry. Where, then, would you have a woman like Aimee Semple McPherson, who started the Four Square Church, and whom God used mightily in her day? He also used Kathryn Kuhlman, as well as many other women we do not have much information about.

I say this: If God did not call the woman, it is not going to work. If God did not call the man, it is not going to work. As an illustration: Sometimes I get letters from Seventh Day Adventists telling us that we should worship God on Saturday. If my worshipping on Sunday was a violation of the Sabbath, and if God was strictly holding what is referred to as the Sabbath day inviolate, there would be no way anyone could get saved under my ministry on a Sunday. It is the Holy Spirit who makes us new creatures in Christ Jesus, and He would be confirming my *disobedience* to the Sabbath day if he allowed people to be saved on Sunday.

I believe women can be anything God calls them to be. If He does not call a woman to be something, then she should not be it. If He calls her, there will be a corresponding anointing for her to stand in the office of whatever God calls her to do — and it will work! The Bible says there is neither male nor female. We are all one in Christ Jesus.

19. *Question:*

What about ministers serving the Lord's Supper without being ordained?

Dr. Price:

That is a personal question. I do not find anything in the Bible, to my recollection, that says it makes any difference who serves it. Every Christian has a right to receive it. If you have a right to receive it, you ought to have a right to serve it.

20. *Question:*

How do you handle a pastoral salary with a growing church?

Dr. Price:

I ask my Board, "How much does it cost you to buy gas?" They tell me, say, $1.50 a gallon. I ask, "How much does it cost you to pay for utilities — electric, gas, and water?" They give me a figure, and I tell them, "That is how much it costs me, too." I have to make the same money anyone else makes, because I have to live in the same world.

You cannot be paid a salary if the church does not have the money. That is for *sure!* However, I feel that when you are in full-time ministry, it means your ministry should be taking care of you, just like your job would if you were in secular employment. If you were making $20,000 a year in secular employment, you probably cannot live off of $10,000 a year working for the church. Until the church can pay you the $20,000 you were making in secular work, you should not go into full-time ministry. Stay on your secular job, then go down to the church evenings, Sundays, or whenever, until the church can pay you.

When I hire an assistant pastor, I always match the salary he was making in the secular world. With the growth of your church, the growth of the finances, and the growth of your particular needs, you have to start somewhere at a given figure. From that point, it is a matter of increases based on the cost of living.

71

We use that as an index for all of our employees. We use the Los Angeles cost of living index, which is one of the highest in the nation. Then we couple it with the United States cost of living index as a place to begin dealing with salary. We hire everyone who works at the church at the same salary he or she would have made in secular industries. It is not fair to ask you to work for the King of all the ages for less than what you make when the devil is paying you.

21. *Question:*

Should a pastor sit down for a year if he has had a sexual relationship outside of marriage?

Dr. Price:

It depends on how you have structured your ministry. After all, who will make him sit down? Himself? The Board? At Crenshaw, we have certain guidelines we go by. For instance, if a female choir member plays the fool and lets a man get her pregnant, right away, both the man and the woman have to sit down. The male has to sit down for a year before he can be reinstated in any auxiliary or Helps Ministry, and he has to be visible and participating at the church, so we can see he has repented. The woman has to go ahead and have the baby, then has to sit down until one year after the baby is born.

If I had an assistant pastor who was in a sexual situation, I probably would have to let him go. I would not turn him out of church, but he could not be in the office of assistant pastor. Therefore, he could not sit down, because he would not have any income. I would have to let him go so he could get a job and take care of his family.

As for a pastor — again, I do not know who is going to sit him down. I think there should be a time for repentance, so maybe he should sit himself down. He needs to do *something!* He cannot keep ministering, especially if it becomes public knowledge. Even if you repent instantly, and it is honest, true repentance, other people cannot see your heart, so there should be, perhaps, a minimum of at least a year in which you would have to sit down.

Usually, when a pastor commits adultery or something like that, and the congregation knows it, most of the people leave, anyway. My wife and I have gone to many churches where they were packed at one time, and almost empty when we returned, because the pastor had messed up. A pastor has to make rules for himself so he will not get into a situation like that, because it can be very hard to come back after something like that. My best advice is this: DON'T MESS UP!

22. *Question:*

What do you do if the pastor's wife is unfaithful to the pastor, and the church knows it?

Dr. Price:

If there are enough people who know it, then I would suggest that the people get together as a delegation, go to the pastor and inform him of it. If the pastor knows about it, he needs to be put in a position to make a decision about it. Because the knowledge of what the wife is doing will DESTROY the church, and destroy other lambs who come to the ministry. IF YOU LOVE THE PERSON, GO TO THEM, SIT DOWN TOGETHER, AND TALK.

However, make SURE that YOU KNOW THAT YOU KNOW! The only way you can be sure is by having eyewitnesses. DO NOT accuse someone of something only because you *suspect* it, because you can easily destroy someone's life with what you say.

When I was a young minister, we had a pastor who was teaching us on this subject, and he used this illustration. When this pastor went to a certain area to minister, some people came to him about a lady who was prominent in the church, but who was living with a man and was not married to him. The pastor, being a dutiful man, and wanting to do everything right, decided to pay a pastoral visit to these people.

He came to the house where these people lived, and the woman was home and she invited him in. It was a very hot area of the country, and it was summertime, so the woman asked if the pastor would like some lemonade. He said, "Oh, yes, that would be nice." While she was getting the lemonade, he noticed there were some pictures and plaques on the wall — *and one of the plaques was a marriage certificate.*

If the pastor had gone over there and accused that lady because of some bogus information, he could have destroyed someone's life. BE SURE you know what you are talking about, and that you have some hard evidence, before you approach ANYONE about it.

23. *Question:* How should a pastor's wife handle a woman who is always in her husband's face?

Betty Price:

That is a good question, because women love to be in your husband's face. I had only one experience with this, and it was one to last me for life. If you take your place, and not be afraid, you will not ever have to go through situations like that. When we were young in the ministry, we had a woman who would always want to minister to Fred from a spiritual standpoint. She was always telling him spiritual things, and had a prophecy for him every hour on the hour every day. We had just started moving in the Spirit, so I did not want to hinder Fred spiritually, but it got to be too much. I finally said, "No way!" At first, Fred really did not understand the situation. He was innocent, and he was interested in spiritual things at the time. BUT THAT IS HOW YOU CAN GET TRAPPED. You have to be strong enough to stand up and say, "I don't care what anyone else thinks.

I don't like it, and it's bothering me. Even if I'm wrong, quit it, because I am your wife." After I told Fred, he made a decision, and he has never talked to that woman since.

24. *Question:*

Betty, do you always submit to Fred when he wants you sexually, even when you are very tired and he is not — because it seems like a man is never too tired to make love?

Betty Price:

No, I would not say that I always submit, and I think a husband should be understanding. If you are a good wife, when that time comes when you are really tired, if your husband is right, he will understand. We have had times when we both used wisdom and just waited. The Bible says, ...**Submitting yourselves TO ONE ANOTHER.** It is not just the wife who should be sensitive, but the husband also. I believe that if you grow together and are in one accord, you will know when and when not to wait.

25. *Question:*

How do you deal with a pastor who has a split personality? In public he is a knight in shining armor; at home, he is like Frankenstein's monster.

Dr. Price:

You have a couple of choices. You can personally talk to him about it. And if that does not work, there is another thing you can do, which will take a lot of boldness and a lot of love. EXPOSE HIM TO THE CONGREGATION!

If he is Frankenstein's monster, he does not have any business in the pulpit, anyway. If he is not practicing what he preaches, he has NO RIGHT telling anyone else how to live. Our lives are supposed to be above reproach. Anything you think you know on me, tell it. As Paul said, *Follow me as I follow Christ.* If a man cannot say that, he has no business being a pastor. The devil will see that it is exposed one of these days, so it is better that you expose it now.

26. *Question:*

How do you handle the training of new members in your church?

Dr. Price:

We have what is called a New Members' Class. I saw the need a long time ago for some type of buffer zone between the time people come into the ministry, and the time they become bona fide members of the church. Also, I saw that people needed to be grounded. Along with the people who were being born again and entering the family of God, there were many others who had been drifting along, and were extremely hungry for the things of God.

Many times, they wanted to put the same traditions and non-scriptural beliefs on Crenshaw that they had practiced in their former churches.

I wanted them to know right from the gate that we are not at their former churches. I wanted them to find out how we do everything here. Therefore, I started the New Members' Class. It is a four-lesson program, and no person who makes application for membership at our church is placed on the active membership roll until they complete the New Members' program.

The four-week class deals with the basics of Christianity: salvation, being filled with the Spirit, giving tithes and offerings, etc. We also teach them about how the church is governed and how it operates, so that they will know what they are into. The class is basically a primer to get them started on studying these areas on their own.

At the end of the fourth class, the Right-Hand of Fellowship is automatically extended to people who have completed the class. They then have the option of coming up to shake the hands of the Executive Board and myself on the first Sunday of the month. Whether or not they exercise that option, their names are placed on the active membership roll of the church, and at that point, I feel they are INFORMED members.

One of my assistant pastors teaches the class. I cannot do it because the church is too large. As I said, I knew a long time ago that I needed the class; however, I did not have the personnel to handle it. When the right time came, and the right person came along, I turned it over to him. The class is taught before the Sunday morning service, and we also have the lessons on videotape, so that people who cannot come to the Sunday class can make up the lessons during the week.

27. *Question:*

Do you have a follow-up on the new convert before he joins the New Members' Class?

Dr. Price:

No. We give an invitation at all our worship services and Bible studies for people to come and receive Christ. When they come forward, they are taken into the counseling room. One of the personal workers sits down and ministers to each of the people. The worker explains the Word of God to them concerning salvation, and we leave it at that.

Many times, the person being ministered to decides that he wants to accept Christ as his Savior, and that he also wants to become a member of Crenshaw Christian Center. The personal minister will minister about salvation, lead that person into receiving Christ, and show him from the Word how to base his relationship with God on the Word of God by faith, rather than by feelings or emotions.

They will then be encouraged to go to the New Members' Class. At the same time, they will be told they are not members, and that they will not be considered members until they complete the class. We then, of course, tell them when the class meets, and encourage them to get started in that direction. That is all we do about that.

28. *Question:*

I am just starting a ministry, and I would like any information I can get on starting a church.

Dr. Price:

When you say that, it all depends on whether you are talking about the legal aspects of incorporating, or, in terms of organizing a church, what kind of officers you need, whether or not you need elders, etc. Much of it depends on what the Lord has called you to do, because every church does not have to be a carbon copy of every other church, in terms of its organization. It depends on the vision you have, and the kind of person you are.

There will be some basic things you will have to have. In California, for example, to qualify — or to be recognized by the state and federal governments you have to be incorporated. That means you must have certain officers in your corporate structure — a president, a vice-president, a secretary, and a treasurer. The secretary and the treasurer can be the same person, so you need at least three officers to qualify for incorporation.

As for your church structure, your church will be governed and controlled according to the constitution, set of by-laws or both, that you come up with. There is no carbon copy of that. It is whatever works best for you.

When I started out, I did not know anything about organizing a church. The Lord opened some doors for me to become involved with Melodyland Christian Center in Anaheim, California, in terms of ministering, and the pastor there gave me permission to take one of their constitutions and by-laws. I examined them very carefully. There were many things in their constitution I did not want to do or felt would not fit me, so I deleted them, then added and rearranged from there. It was not copyrighted, so I used it as a skeletal outline, then put the "meat on the bones," so to speak, that I wanted on it.

When it comes to starting a ministry, the first thing to do is FIND OUT WHAT GOD WANTS YOU TO DO, and let Him direct you as to how you should start your ministry. There are many people pastoring who have no business pastoring, because they never waited on God to direct them. God may be calling you to go work for someone else. In fact, your calling may be to be an assistant the rest of your life. That is a legitimate calling.

As far as some technical things are concerned, you can ask someone, but everything should be specifically based on what you are, and what you are going to do.

29. *Question:*

What kind of church government do you think God is pleased with under the New Testament, such as independent, eldership, congregational? And why that type?

Dr. Price:

First of all, whatever works best for you. Secondly, as I stated previously, if you are a non-profit corporation of the state of California, recognized as such by the state and the federal governments for income tax purposes, there are certain things you have to incorporate into the government of your church. Otherwise, you will have some problems with the government. The government will watch you like a hawk, because it does not want another "church" or "ministry" operating simply to gouge people out of their money.

At my church, we have elders and deacons. The elders — who are ministers — are appointed by me and ratified by the Executive Board, while the deacons are elected by and from the congregation. Deacons deal with the temporal aspect of the church, while the elders deal with the spiritual aspect — ministry of the Word. We also have an Executive Board, which is made up of our six deacons, three of the elders, a secretary, a treasurer, and myself — 12 people all together. The Board runs the church. It spends money, launches programs, and so on.

Three deacons are elected for a one-year period, and the other three are elected for a two-year period, the theory being that you will always have experienced men on the Board. A person can serve only two terms, then he has to go off the Board for one year before he can run again. Also, while the deacons are elected by the congregation, our constitution provides for a nominating committee, which is made up of the pastor, one elder, and one deacon.

We place in nomination at least two names for every office to be filled, because we want to give the people a choice. For instance, if all six offices are up for grabs, we will usually find at least 12 people to place in nomination. But we also have other parameters we consider.

First, a nominee has to be a tither. No man who is unwilling to tithe has any business talking about how my tithe should be spent.

They also have to be family men, with their families in order. They have to be highly visible people, Word people, filled with the Spirit and speaking with other tongues, as outlined in Acts 2:4. Finally, they must have a good report in the congregation.

The nominating committee will find 12 men who fit these criteria. At election time, we make up a ballot with the 12 men's names on it, and tell the people to vote for six of these men. That allows God to bring into office the six men who should be there, and at the same time allows the congregation to have a part in electing these people to serve them. The election results are announced at our annual progress report meeting, where we also present a financial statement, a financial report, and a ministry report to the congregation.

30. *Question:*

At Crenshaw, you have what is called Helps Ministry. What does the word "helps" mean?

Dr. Price:

A general definition of "helps" would be anything that would allow a person to render a help to a ministry. For instance, there is nothing in the Bible about having an usher board, but believe me, if you have a Sunday morning congregation of 5,000 people, you need ushers. Therefore, someone who is an usher would be a help. There is also nothing in the Bible about having a choir in the church. However, a choir could render a ministry of help in terms of ministering to the people in song, thereby setting the stage for the reception of the spoken Word.

Even a person who stands in a ministerial office can be a help. Example: I personally, as a pastor and teacher, am a helps ministry to other ministries in various ways. I can be a financial help by making contributions to other ministries to help support them. I can also be a ministry of helps in the sense of ministering in another ministry's meeting. As I do that, I am helping that ministry.

The ministry of helps, governments, and diversities of tongues (1 Cor. 12:28) operates in the ministry of a pastor, and in that sense, the local pastor can be a help. He can be a help to an evangelist. The evangelist may need a place of operation. He may need a place to run his monies through, so that he can be under the covering of the non-profit status of that pastor and that church.

31. *Question:*

If I were a member of Crenshaw, and I wanted to become an usher or a Sunday school teacher, or join the choir, what requirements have been set up that I would have to meet?

Dr. Price:

At our church, to join the Helps Ministry — which is what we have those and other departments grouped under — after you have completed the New Members' class and received the Right-Hand of Fellowship, you have to sit down in the congregation for one year before you can apply. That way, you can get an idea of where the ministry is going, how we operate, and also get enough of the Word into you so that when you get into the Helps Ministry, you will be a help and not a hindrance. If you do not know which way we are going, you may dream up your own way to go. We would then have people in Helps Ministry at cross purposes with one another.

When a person applies for a Helps Ministry position, he fills out an application form, just like you would fill out an application form for a job, because I believe the day is long gone when we have people in the congregation in the public eye who are leaders, but are not living as they should. After all, the television camera may flash on a person in the choir, and a viewer may recognize that person as someone he gets drunk with every Saturday night. Consequently, that viewer may assume I am not for real, because I have someone like that singing in my choir.

Leadership does not end in the pulpit. In my opinion, a leader is anyone who stands in a position of representing the church, whether that person is a Sunday school teacher, a hostess, or a greeter out on the church grounds. Therefore, on the application, we ask questions about the person's morality and different things like that. If they want to lie, fine, but they will soon be found out, anyway. There is also what we call a "moral interview," in which we review the application with the applicant, and he also has to attend an orientation session before he can become part of the Helps Ministry.

32. *Question:*

How specific are the requirements you have for being involved in a Helps Ministry? I know the traditional things — like no smoking, no drinking, and spending time in the Word and in prayer. But how specific do you get on those kinds of issues?

Dr. Price:

Just as specific as you have mentioned. No smoking, no drinking, no fornicating, no living together like you are married when you are not married — all the basic moral things. I even go so far as to require that you have a valid driver's license if you drive a car, as well as proof that you have liability insurance.

As for time in prayer and time in the Word, we cannot regulate that, simply because we cannot be with them 24 hours a day. However, we tell them what we expect from a spiritual point of view, in terms of time in the Word, but it is up to them. They will actually be the real losers if they do not take the time, but we certainly emphasize that they *should* do it.

33. *Question:*

What would your advice be to a church that wants to implement a policy of having its new members wait under the Word for a year before applying for a Helps position, but which already has a set structure of ushers and other workers? Do you say, "All of you who are here now, stay in your positions, but starting from this day, there is a new standard?" Or do you disband everything and say, "We are going to start from scratch"?

Dr. Price:

You could do one or the other of those things — or both of them. It all depends on how many people you are talking about, what kind of rules you had before, and what kind of rules you are instituting now.

For example, let us say that before, anyone who wanted to be in Helps Ministry had to go through a one-week New Members' class. Now you are going to change it. So, from now on, beginning on a certain date, you will have a 10-week New Members' class. Everyone who went through the one-week program would be fine, but if anyone else wants to come aboard, he has to go through the 10-week program.

You would not necessarily have to kick everyone out of the positions they have now, unless they are not doing what you want them to do, and you are dissatisfied. If you were dissatisfied, you would then scrap the whole program, and say, "This is what we are going to do from now on. Here are the requirements. If you meet the requirements, you can come back. If not, then you start over, and do thus-and-so."

34. *Question:*

When I have taught the full Gospel, I have had children from the ages of five to 18 years being saved and filled with the Spirit. Many times, those children then go home and do not quite understand what is going on, and the parents come back, saying, "You have my child hypnotized." How can you prepare the children for how the parents may react?

Dr. Price:

Give them the Word. You cannot change anything at home. You will have to inform the children to be as wise as they can, and their parents may not understand what has happened to them because everyone is not ready to hear about being saved, and not everyone wants it. For that reason tell them to use caution.

They should not just go running in talking about a lot of things, but keep it to themselves. When the situation arises and the Spirit of God directs them, they can then speak to their parents about it. Until then, you should add, be careful, be wise, and if their parents do not understand, to just pray by themselves when they are alone, and not talk about being saved or filled with the Holy Ghost unless their parents ask about it.

YOU have the responsibility in this situation to teach the children. But you cannot refrain from teaching the whole counsel of God simply because a parent, relative, friend, or someone else may object. Trust the Lord that, by the Spirit in them, wisdom will prevail and they will know how to handle themselves, so that they will not get into bad situations that will totally discourage them.

35. *Question:*

My husband and I write for a leading Black newspaper, and we get a great response from our Black men who are incarcerated. They tell us, ''I'm coming home. I want fellowship. I want friendship. I have been saved since I've been in prison. What can you offer me?'' And many of the churches are not really ready for these Black men once they are out, because they are afraid; some of the men have committed murder.

How can we go about telling our church to accept these men, because many times, your members will leave if they know you are allowing ex-convicts to come to the house of the Lord? What should be our plan of action?

Dr. Price:

Here is one man's opinion. I do not really see that we need a "plan." If a person comes to Crenshaw, we do not care where they come from, or how they come. We do not even ask them where they come from, we just present the Gospel to them. We have had people who have come to our congregation who have been in all sorts of things, and have had all kinds of problems in society. And, to my knowledge, we have not had any problem.

The worst thing you can do, I believe, is stand a man up in the congregation and tell everyone, ''This man has killed 19 people, raped 14, and has had incestuous relationships with his mother and his children over the years. We just want you to welcome him in, and treat him as a brother!'' Some people may leave if you do something like *that!*

People have also written us letters like the ones you receive, and we tell them, ''Come on in and get in the flow. You do not need to tell anyone you are from prison. Just come on in and receive.'' And they do just that. We do not care where they come from, because the Church is God's laundry on earth, and any dirty clothes ought to go to the laundry to get cleaned up. We welcome anyone.

36. *Question:*

Does the pastor tithe from his income to his own church, or to another ministry? And does the pastor tithe from the church's tithes and offerings, and if so, to where?

Dr. Price:

The Bible does not tell you to tithe into another ministry. It is all right if you want to do it, but do not get in bondage to it. You are supposed to tithe to the storehouse — and the other ministry is not necessarily your storehouse. If you are receiving from your church, you ought to tithe to it. If it is not good enough for YOU to tithe to, who else will tithe to it?

Also, you do not need to tithe the church's tithes or offerings anywhere. You can give if you want to, but you do not have to tithe. We do not tithe to any other ministry, but we give as we are led by the Spirit to other ministries. There is nothing in the Bible about one ministry tithing to another, but if you find a ministry worth tithing into, go ahead. But do not get in bondage to it.

37. *Question:*

How do you get your people involved in tithing?

Dr. Price:

You teach them by precept, and by example. You have to TEACH tithing — and you need to find out about it before you teach it, because otherwise, you will put the people in bondage. And, most importantly, you have to BE a tither. Never ask your people to do something you will not do. If you are not ready to do it, do not tell them about it, because you will not do it with any conviction. Through the Spirit, they will know you are phony.

38. *Question:*

Should we wait for God to send teachers before starting up a children's church?

Dr. Price:

That is an excellent question, and it is something you can apply to an usher board, hostess or host committee, or any auxiliary or organization in the church. For a long time, I did not have ushers, or a head usher, just men who I knew were in the congregation every week to do the job of an usher. I would say, "Brother, would you please take that basket down there, and pass it down?"

I did that until I had someone to work as a head usher. I knew I could not do it, because I had to give myself to the teaching of the Word, so I waited for God to send me the right person. I did the same thing with the Men's Fellowship. We needed a Men's Fellowship, but I did not do anything until I had someone to lead it. I do not start any auxiliary of the church until I have someone to put over it who can take care of it, because I cannot take care of it and give myself to the teaching of the Word.

You do not need to have ushers. You do not need to have a Sunday school, or a children's church. The only thing you have to do is to feed the sheep and feed the lambs. You can bring the kids and the parents together in one room and feed them. It is nice to departmentalize, if you have the resources and the people.

But do it when you CAN, based upon having people you can trust and are qualified, as far as you are concerned, to fulfill your vision. Other than that, do not let anyone pressure you into thinking you have to have this, and you have to have that.

39. *Question:*

Are you familiar with the term "Co-dependency"? If so, in relation to being a Christian and our confession of faith, how do we deal with this? Also, for those who are dependent on drugs, alcohol, or other things, how do we deal with the confession of that dependency?

Dr. Price:

For those who are dependent, one thing I would do is not have them confess dependency on the things you mentioned. Personally, I believe the key to all our problems is God's Word BELIEVED, CONFESSED, *and* APPLIED to one's life.

The only thing I know to do is to teach people what the Word says about who they are in Christ. The bottom line then is that THEY have to do something about it. Even if you have a drug program such as the one we have, and you get together to fellowship and support one another, the bottom line still has to be an individual decision on the part of the person to abstain from whatever it is that person is dependent upon.

I would not confirm a dependent person in his dependency by having him confess, "I'm dependent on drugs," or, "I'm dependent on alcohol." Rather, I would teach them to CONFESS WHAT THE WORD says. *That* will break the dependency, if they really want to be free, because faith comes by hearing, and hearing by the Word of God. If they keep SAYING it long enough, they will start BELIEVING it, and it will BREAK that power, because the power of the Word of God can break anything.

In the process of teaching them that, you may have to coddle those people a little bit. You may have to make out over them some, and hug and kiss them a little, and perhaps get them together with other Christians like them for some mutual strengthening, because those things may be what they need.

However, the bottom line is, do not confess they are dependent persons, but that they are FREE from the dependency, according to the Word of God.

40. *Question:*

How do you properly take care of an invited guest speaker?

Dr. Price:

I take the attitude that number one, I would treat someone like I want to be treated. Then, in terms of ministry, that minister is a representative of Jesus. So how would I treat Jesus if He were physically here and I were inviting him to be a speaker at my convention or at my church, etc.? How would you treat Jesus?

We are the Body of Christ. He is the Head. We are the Body, so I am just as much Jesus as Jesus is, and we need to see that. And if we would really see that, we would stop mistreating one another and stop acting unethically in many of our activities.

How would you transport Jesus? Would you transport Him around in some broken-down automobile? Would you rent a limousine and have him picked up in style if no other decent automobile were available? How would you treat

Jesus? You would treat Him with respect, with honor, with dignity. You would show Him the best that you had, and that is how we ought to treat each other, no matter who it is. What kind of honorarium would you give Him? All you have to do is treat everyone else the same way. If you do that, then you will be operating ethically, and you will be blessed for it, because you are doing it as unto the Lord. That is the way I see it. And that is the way I attempt to do it.

41. *Question:*

Should you make his or her flight arrangements and send him or her the ticket?

Dr. Price:

There is no hard set rule. There is no right and wrong way to do it. It is what works best for you. I do not buy anyone's ticket and send them the ticket, because I do not want anyone buying my ticket and sending me the ticket. I tell my speaker, "We will provide you with roundtrip, first-class airfare from your home port to us and back again. Now if you want to take a circuit ride and go to four or five other cities, that's fine; it's up to you. You do that on your own. But we're going to pay for you from New York to California and back to New York first class."

I let them know they can get their own ticket; they might have their own travel agent and might want to make their own arrangements. I do, because it's very important to me where I sit on an airplane.

42. *Question:*

Should you offer hotel accommodations or open up your home to your invited guest?

Dr. Price:

Once again, there is no hard set rule. It all depends on you and your circumstances at the time you invite someone. And it also depends upon the person that you are inviting. In some cases, you might have him in your home; in other situations, you might have him in a hotel. I'm a private person. I like my privacy. So I prefer staying in a hotel. That's me. For some people, it doesn't matter. So, you need to find out what his preference is.

43. *Question:*

Dr. Price, prosperity is relative. What if your ministry is not in a position where a first-class air flight is in the picture, but you want to have the speaker and he says he really wouldn't mind flying coach?
Dr. Price:

Definitely everything is relative to where you are. In some situations, the point that was brought up also lets you know that maybe you don't need a speaker any way. If you cannot afford the Cadillac upkeep, maybe you don't need one. So you have to consider that, too.

At Crenshaw Christian Center, we didn't have that many speakers until we were able to afford what it takes to treat a speaker like we feel he should be treated. The point is, give whatever best you have to offer. Jesus would not expect you to go out and get a 747 Jumbo Jet to fly Him here when you could fly Him in a smaller aircraft where He would still be very comfortable. What is most important is — just let it be the very *best* you have. Do not treat your speakers as though they do not matter.

44. *Question:*

What is your wife's role in the church, other than to support you?
Dr. Price:

I have never required my wife to do anything in church. Some pastors put a lot of pressure on their wives to make them fit into a role they are not qualified to fit in: (1) They do not want to be in that role, (2) they do not like to be in the limelight, and (3) they are the kind of person who stays in the background and supports from behind. In many churches, there is the idea that the pastor's wife has to be the head of this committee, the head of that group, and play the piano and direct the choir on Sunday as well.

In the Bible, God does not say He is going to give the church a helpmeet. He says He is going to give ME a helpmeet. So my wife is to help ME, not the church. If I want her to do something that is involved in the church, that will help me. But her doing that has to be based on what I feel I need her to do — and then give her the opportunity to choose whether or not SHE wants to do it — and not get ugly if she *does not* want to do it.

For years, Betty did not do anything, as far as being actively involved with the workings of the ministry. She came to the meetings, she supported me, she was visibly there, but I did not say, "You have to do this, that, and the other."

Betty became actively involved based on needs. She saw a particular need, so she became responsible for the Women's Fellowship. At first, she ran it, but then she appointed presidents to be in charge and she became the advisor. She would oversee the Fellowship to make sure everything was working as it ought to work. I let her do that because it was what she wanted to do, not because I required her to do it. I required her to take care of me and the children — that was it.

Do not make your spouse something YOU want her to be. Let her find her own place. That way, she will be more supportive, and she will be able to do it more easily. It depends on the talents the wife has, but do not expect her to do something just because she is the pastor's wife.

The main place a wife needs to be is by her husband's side. That, in itself, will be a deterrent to many things the devil will try to do in that ministry. She does not have to say anything. As long as she is with her husband, that will deter many things. She does not even have to be seen at every meeting, but if it is what the two of you agree upon, that is fine.

45. *Question:*

I have a 16-year-old daughter, and she likes worldly music, dances, and parties. She is the typical worldly child. We have no problem with her attending church on Sunday, but if we want her to go to other services, it is a case of bending her arm to come. On top of that, most of her friends do not go to church. We have not always been in ministry, and we have made many mistakes along the way. We let her listen to the music and go to school dances and parties because when we refuse to let her go, there is a lot of rebellion and depression. As far as the parents go, is there a limitation we should put on this?

Dr. Price:

This is a difficult question, because every parent is different, and every child is different. Everything goes back to where you started and how you raised your children up to a certain point, even to when you entered ministry, and when you became a Christian. I think it is rather difficult to say, "You should do this, and you should do that." You will have to seek the Lord as to how to deal with your child, because that child is your creation.

Whatever that child is, YOU created that child by the environment you provided for her. From my experience of growing up, I am convinced there is nothing out in the world that can affect your children in a negative way if they have their home together. You have to have rules and regulations in the home, but the APPLICATION of those rules and regulations take WISDOM. I would have to follow you around for a while in your home to more specifically answer your question.

When Betty and I got into the Word, I made instant, radical changes. That was me. I did not taper off. I will either do something, or not do it, and I go full speed as far as making a change in my lifestyle. I sat the family down and told them, "Here is what we were, here is what we are now, and here is where we are going." I then set down the boundary lines of what would and what would not be accepted.

I had a challenge with my oldest daughter when I said that everyone in the family would go to church every Sunday morning and every Sunday night. She wanted to know why we all had to go. Sometimes, you get to the place where you cannot tell someone why. It simply gets down to the case of, "Well, we're going! I'm the daddy! I'm the pastor! We have church at night, we go as a family, and that's it!" She kept asking, "Why, why, why?" and I said, "Look. I said we are going. As long as you are under my roof, breathing my air which I am paying for within the walls of this house, using my water, my electricity, eating my food, you are going to church!"

She said, "I don't want to go to church on Sunday nights." I told her, "I don't care. You don't have to *want* to go, but you are going!"

The church was so small — eight rows — that from the pulpit you could see the whites of everyone's eyes in the back row. My daughter would come in Sunday night to the back row, mad because she did not want to be there. She would sit there, looking like she was ready to burst. The devil tried to tell me, "You are going to warp that child's mind," and I told him, "The Lord told me in the Word to train up a child not in the way the child wants to go, or in the way her friends want to go, but in the way the child *ought* to go, and they will not depart from it."

Many parents give in to pressure from friends, relatives, the sitcoms, you name it, because they are afraid of losing their children. But I did not give in, and I was fair with them. I did not go drink a beer, then tell them they could not drink a Coke. I was consistent down the line.

Because I stayed with it, and because my daughters saw the reality of what I preached on Sunday in my life, God vindicated His Word. All three of my daughters are working in the ministry. They are all married. They were all virgins when they got married. They went to the same schools everyone else went to, with drugs and sex everywhere, and I never had one second's problem with my kids getting involved with those things.

46. *Question:*

I understand you went through personal financial crisis early in the ministry. What caused the failure? What did God show you in leading you out?

Dr. Price:

First of all, I was operating in the curse of the law, because I was robbing God by not tithing. (Mal. 3:8.) That caused all the financial hardship. Immaturity added to that. A lack of knowledge on how to handle money added to that. The bottom line was, I was a disaster going somewhere to happen several times, and all the financial problems we had in our marriage were all my fault.

The biggest key for me to get out of that situation was learning how to walk by faith. I then found out I had God's Word as my guide, and that I was the *master* of my circumstances, not the victim. I took the authority the Word said I had, and began to do what the Lord said, relative to giving. That is, you have to give BEFORE you can receive, and the reason it is more blessed to give than to receive is that the giving CAUSES the receiving to take place. If you do not give, it is impossible to receive. I learned that, and I made a determination to be a tither.

God is not your problem when it comes to finances. YOU ARE! There is no problem when it comes to resources, but God does not drop money out of the sky. The challenge is getting the money into your hands, and then using wealth wisely.

I like to receive big, and I found out that in order to do that, I have to give big! I started out with tithing the standard 10 percent, then at different stages of my development, I would set higher goals — 12-1/2 percent, 15 percent, then 20 percent. Now I give away 25 percent of all my income. The more I give, the more I receive, and the more I receive, the more I give.

You also have to change your attitude about money, because you can tithe and still stay in debt. Here is a principle that will help — not only for finances, but also for being overweight. LOSING WEIGHT and LOSING DEBT IS EASY. The CHALLENGE IS NOT EATING or SPENDING AS MUCH ONCE THE WEIGHT OR DEBT IS GONE.

I used to think when I had a dollar, that I had 100 cents I could spend. When I began tithing, I changed my attitude. I would start thinking that I had only 90 cents I could spend, instead of 100, and that the other 10 cents was God's. As a result of changing my attitude, I HAVE NOT MISSED ONE OPPORTUNITY TO TITHE IN 20 YEARS! NOT ONE TIME, OR HALF A TIME, OR ANY OTHER FRACTION OF A TIME!

When you get that principle into your spiritual craw, you will not obligate yourself to spend everything you make. I could use the money I tithe for other things, but I consider myself only a trustee of the total amount I make until I get God's money over to Him. That is how I have not missed one tithe in 20 years.

As I said before, the same principle works for keeping off weight. You can lose the weight by simply not eating, but if you do not change your mindset about how much you eat once you have lost that weight, you will go back to eating the way you did before, and gain back the weight you lost.

Here is one way you can cut down. Fill up your plate the way you normally do, then before you start eating, take a knife, cut right down the middle of the plate. Scrape half of the food off of the plate, and eat only the half that is left.

47. Question:

You mention that there is a point of progression where you went from tithing 10 percent to where you are now. As I study the Word, it talks about "tithe" meaning tenth. Would you explain where you have the cutoff between tithes and other giving?

Dr. Price:

That is a good question. Tithing is percentage giving, and biblically, it is 10 percent. Once you reach 10 percent, that is the tithe. What I have done is, I have used the principle of percentage to control my giving. I give away 25 percent of my income, but 10 percent is tithes, and 15 percent is offerings. I give the tithe to Crenshaw, because that is my home church, and the offerings I give to Crenshaw projects plus other ministries' projects. I do not divide my tithe and give two percent to one ministry, two percent to another, and two percent to a third ministry, and four percent to Crenshaw. ALL OF THE TITHE must go to the storehouse where you receive the major portion of your spiritual enrichment and education.

Anything over the 10 percent is your money; you can do whatever you want with it. The tithe is God's money. You are not even giving that. You are PAYING a debt, an assessment. THAT IS A REQUIREMENT! It is not unfair, however, because what you get back in return far exceeds the 10 percent. If any finance company in the world gave you the kind of deal God offers us, you would jump at it in a minute. It would be great to invest 10 percent and get back the windows of heaven blessing to the point there will not be room enough to receive it. (Mal. 3:10.)

48. *Question:*

Do I live by faith and postdate a check, or not pay the rent, so I can have money to give to God?

Dr. Price:

Unless you go to a person and explain the situation, you cannot give them a postdated check. If you give someone a postdated check without telling them anything, you will cut your blessings off.

When you give a check, it is the same as giving that person money. There has to be money IN THE BANK AT THE MINUTE YOU WRITE THE CHECK. When you write a check without having money in the bank, you are being dishonest.

If you write the check and the person takes that check to the bank immediately, it will not be cashed, because there is no money in the account to cover the check. You are telling a lie, and you cannot be blessed as long as you are operating that way. In fact, you give Satan a legal right to destroy you, and there is nothing God can do about it.

If you tell the person to whom you are writing the check, that you would like to postdate the check, and that person says it is all right, then it is fine, because *you have made that person aware* of the situation. Normally, however, you must have the money in the bank to cover it. You cannot write a check in the morning, then go to the bank in the afternoon and deposit the money to cover the check. You are lying if you do that, because there was no money in the bank when you wrote the check. Suppose there is a traffic accident on the way to the bank. The streets may be blocked, and you may not be able to get to the bank with the money in time.

Many preachers, like many Christians in general, have this habit. And it is another way they are messing up on receiving the blessings of God.

As for not paying the rent, or any other bill, so that you have money to give to God, that is stupid! When you do that, you have lost your witness, because you tell your creditor that you are a Christian, then do not keep your Word. You made an agreement for him to do something for you — pipe in your gas, water, electricity, or let you live on his property — and in return you would pay the bill. When the bill comes, you decide you will not pay the bill, you will pay God instead. You are NOT keeping your agreement!

If you do not have enough money to pay God AND pay the light bill, you are already overextended and you have no business with either the lights or the tithing. TITHING IS FOR YOUR BENEFIT, NOT FOR GOD'S! If you think about it, not a penny of your tithe goes to God. It goes to the local church, and is fed back to you in services through the church.

If you have not been tithing before now, you already are a God robber. DO NOT START TITHING UNTIL YOU CAN AFFORD TO TITHE.

If you do not pay a bill, you are robbing the people who sent you the bill. That is even worse than robbing God. God will forgive you, but many times, people will not. When you go back later to tell them about Jesus, they will tell you, "Don't tell me anything about Jesus, because you are a liar. Your word is no good, so I can't believe what you say about Jesus."

This is how I began tithing: At the time, I was so enmeshed in debt, I could not save anything. Because as soon as the money came, it was spent. I was working a full-time job, so I went to the accountant at my place of employment, and changed my income tax deduction from four dependents to zero. At the end of that year, I had a refund coming. When I got my refund, I looked over the array of bills I had, figured out which bill approximated what

I would give on a monthly basis in tithing, then I took the refund and paid off that bill in one lump sum. In place of the monthly payment on that bill, I started tithing, and since then, I have never changed.

That was 25 years ago. I began tithing out of an obligation, and out of fear of the statement, ''Will a man rob God?'' Five years later, I got into the Word, and found out the benefit of tithing and how to walk by faith.

I knew at that point that if I could get the windows of heaven blessing, I could pay off my other bills — along with NOT adding anything else to the account. I decided then, NO MORE BUYING! Eating makes fat, and buying makes debt. We had an account for absolute emergencies, but other than that, we did not buy anything. For two years, I did not even buy a Christmas tree. I love Christmas trees, but there was no point in buying one when we did not have the extra money for it. We did no extra spending until we reached our goal, and when we reached our goal, we did not have to do without anything else anymore.

Do not neglect to pay a bill so you can tithe. If you cannot pay your bills and tithe, you are not ready for tithing. Give a dollar as an offering, and believe God for the return on the dollar. When the return comes, do not spend it. Act like you do not have it, and apply it to one of your bills. Liquidate that bill, and rearrange your finances so that, within the framework of the money you have available, you can start tithing.

As I said, you may be robbing God already. However, God is gracious and merciful. When you do not know you are robbing God, He will put up with it. What God will *not* put up with is when you rob Him deliberately. When I was robbing God, I did not know I was robbing Him, because the church I attended did not tell me about tithing. I was doing it in ignorance. God knew that, and He was merciful to me. If I stop tithing now, I have no excuse. He will hold me accountable for every jot and tittle.

49. *Question:*

Where is the balance between faith and foolishness?

Dr. Price:

Faith is always acting in line with what the Word says. Foolishness is doing something contrary to the Word. The Bible tells us that they who do not take care of their own houses are not worthy. If you cannot take care of your house, you cannot take care of the church of God. I take care of my home, then I take care of the things that belong to God. The home is second, the ministry is third. Many ministers have that in reverse order. When you always act in accordance with the Word, you are always in balance.

50. *Question:*

Once a church is sent out from a ministry, do you feel that church is obligated to pay its home church a tithe from its income?

Dr. Price:

Let me qualify that. If Crenshaw Christian Center started a satellite church in Pasadena, California, for example, and I send one of my assistant pastors to pastor the church, then that church is Crenshaw Christian Center. All of our monies would be one, and we would simply be responsible for taking care of the expenses.

However, let us say one of my assistant pastors is led of the Lord to leave and start his own ministry. We would send him off, say, "Praise the Lord!" and he would not have to send us anything. There would be no obligation for him to do so. He may need to keep all that he has to meet the expenses of his own ministry.

In Conclusion

Those are just a few pointers I have found beneficial to me in my ministry, and I believe you may find them helpful to you as well.

As I stated in the beginning of this book, all of these suggestions can work in the life of any Christian, as well as in the life of a minister. But I have zeroed in on YOU — the *minister* — to whet your appetite and to goad you into thinking anew and afresh about being successful in the ministry to which God has called you.

Dr. Frederick K.C. Price founded Crenshaw Christian Center in Los Angeles, California in 1973 with a congregation of approximately 300 people. Today, the church has a membership well over 12,000, consisting of persons from varied racial backgrounds.

Crenshaw Christian Center, home of the renowned 10,140-seat FaithDome — the largest church sanctuary in America — has a staff of some 200 employees. CCC, as it is commonly referred to, consists of a School of Ministry, School of the Bible, a Helps Ministry Summer School, the Frederick K.C. Price, III Elementary and Junior High School, and a Child Care Center.

"Ever Increasing Faith" television and radio broadcasts are outreaches of Crenshaw Christian Center. The television program is viewed on more than 100 stations throughout the United States and overseas. And the radio program is broadcast on more than 50 stations nationwide.

Dr. Price travels extensively teaching the WORD OF FAITH simply, making it clear, understandable, and relevant to the daily lives of millions through the power of the Holy Spirit. He is the author of numerous books on faith and divine healing, in addition to other subjects.

In 1990, Dr. Price founded the FELLOWSHIP OF INNER-CITY WORD OF FAITH MINISTRIES (FICWFM), for the purpose of fostering and spreading the faith message among independent ministries located in the urban, metropolitan areas of the United States.

For a complete list of tapes and books by Fred Price, or to receive his publication, *Ever Increasing Faith Messenger*, write:

Fred Price
Crenshaw Christian Center
P. O. Box 90000
Los Angeles, CA 90009

Books by Fred Price

Marriage and the Family
Practical Insight for Family Living

High Finance
God's Financial Plan
Tithes and Offerings

Homosexuality
State of Mind or State of Birth?

Living in the Realm of the Spirit

Is Healing for All?

Now Faith Is

How Faith Works
(also available in Spanish)

How To Obtain Strong Faith
Six Principles

The Holy Spirit — The Missing Ingredient

Faith, Foolishness, or Presumption?

Thank God for Everything?

Explanation To Receiving Your Healing
by the Laying on of Hands

How To Believe God for a Mate

The Origin of Satan

**Available from your local bookstore,
or by writing:**

Harrison House
P. O. Box 35035
Tulsa, OK 74153

For additional copies
of this book
in Canada contact:

Word Alive
P. O. Box 284
Niverville, Manitoba
CANADA R0A 1E0

For international sales in Europe,
contact:

Harrison House Europe
Belruptstrasse 42 A
A — 6900 Bregenz
AUSTRIA

The Harrison House Vision

Proclaiming the truth and the power
Of the Gospel of Jesus Christ
With excellence;

Challenging Christians to
Live victoriously,
Grow spiritually,
Know God Intimately.